Children's
BOOK OF
MUSIC

DK

A DORLING KINDERSLEY BOOK

LONDON, NEW YORK,
MELBOURNE, MUNICH, and DELHI

Senior editor Deborah Lock
Senior designer Hedi Hunter
Additional editing by Penny Smith, Holly
Beaumont, Eleanor Greenwood, Fleur Star
Additional design by Clare Marshall,
Mary Sandberg, Pamela Shiels,
Olga Zavadska, Karen Hood
Art director Martin Wilson
Publishing manager Bridget Giles
Production editor Sean Daly
Production controller Claire Pearson
Jacket designer Martin Wilson
Jacket editor Matilda Gollon
Picture researchers Myriam Mégharbi,
Sarah Hopper

Music consultants
Richard Mallett
Education and Community Producer,
London Philharmonic Orchestra, UK

Ann Marie Stanley
Assistant Professor of Music
Education, Eastman School of Music,
University of Rochester, USA

First published in Great Britain in 2010 by
Dorling Kindersley Limited
80 Strand, London WC2R 0RL

Copyright © 2010 Dorling Kindersley Limited,
A Penguin Company

2 4 6 8 10 9 7 5 3 1
175937 – 07/10

A CIP catalogue record for this book
is available from the British Library.

ISBN 978-1-40535-685-5

Colour reproduction by Media Development
Printing Ltd, UK
Printed and bound by Leo, China

Discover more at
www.dk.com

*Look for this sign,
which gives a track
number for the CD.
Listen to and experience
extracts of music
mentioned in the book
and try out some fun
music-related activities.*

How to use this book

In this book, find out about different
musical styles, the works and lives of
famous composers and performers, how
to play instruments, and the amazing range
of music around the world. There are four
different types of pages in this book:

*MUSICIAN PROFILE: Learn about the life of a
famous composer or performer and discover
the inspiration behind their work.*

*INSTRUMENT PROFILE: Take a close-up look
at the parts of an instrument. Find out how
it's played, its history, and the top players.*

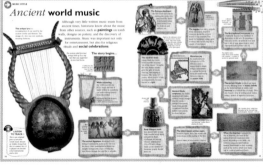

*MUSIC STYLE: Find out about the different
styles of music and the timeline of changing
styles through music history.*

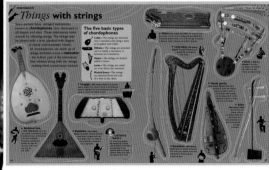

*PERFORMANCE: Marvel at these international
collections of instruments and musical
performances throughout music history.*

Contents

What is **music?**

Everyone reacts to music in a different way because it can be so many things:

It's not just a **tune**

… but can also be a **story**, a **dance**, a **drama**, a **nation's PRIDE**.

It's not just a **STeAdY bEAT**

… but can also be **up-beat**, **jazzy**, **hard rock**, and **hip hop**.

It's not just **one sound**

… but can also be a **duet**, a symphony **orchestra**, a **chOrus**, in fact, there are so many in**STRument**s and *voices* to listen to and blend together.

It's not just a **composition**

… but there's music all around you in the **birds** singing, the patter of **feet**, the clapping of **hands**, and **water** flowing.

"Music produces a type of pleasure that human nature cannot do without." Confucius (c. 551–479 BCE) – Chinese philosopher

It's not just PLEASANT

... but can also be **dramatic**, **spiritual**, **rebellious**, **controversial**, and makes you feel so many **emotions**.

It's not just a **live performance**

... but also on the **radio**, used on the **TV** and in **films**, in fact, you can take it with you on a **portable player**.

It's not just heard in **concert halls**

... but also in **religious buildings**, at **festivals**, on the **streets**, and it's even played in **shops**.

It's not just by someone famous

... but can also be **tribal**, **experimental**, in fact, **you** can create music, too! So, why not have a go!

Early music

(50,000 BCE–1600 CE)

Music has been, and always will be, part of the **cultural identity** of countries around the world. Instruments have been created in many shapes and sizes to make **distinctive** sounds.

From the first *hum*

The first melodies and rhythms of early people were inspired by the noises that they heard around them, such as the **natural sounds** of animals and water, or the banging of their stone tools. Music became a way of communicating, entertaining, celebrating, or working efficiently. **Tribal music** was not written but passed down orally from generation to generation.

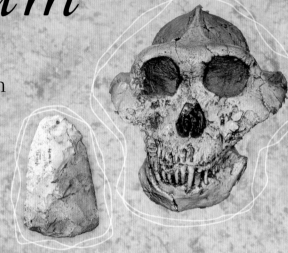

▲ *Sounds of the Neanderthals,* 2009, **Simon Thorne** The Welsh composer Thorne joined up with a team of scientists and anthropologists to reconstruct the musical sounds that the Neanderthals (early humans) might have made using their voices and their flint tools.

▶ Toe-bone whistle, **40,000 BCE, France** Whistles made from the toe bones of animals, such as reindeer, have been discovered while excavating many early people sites.

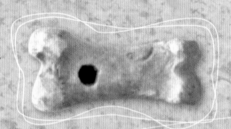

▲ Clapping, **Solomon Islands** Along with singing, hand gestures, rhythmic clapping, and dance movements were an important part of tribal music.

▼ Shaman, **Altai Republic, Russia** In a trance-like state, a shaman would mimic natural sounds, such as those made by a polar bear, bird, or wolf, to communicate with the spirit world.

▲ Divje Babe flute, 40,000 BCE, **Slovenia** This flute, made from animal bones, was found in a cave in Slovenia and is one of the oldest surviving musical instruments.

MUSIC AT HOME:
Listen to the sounds around you at home from the humming of the fridge to the ticking of a clock. What rhythms and melodies can you create with objects around your home, such as pans, shoes, and pencils?

◀ **Katajjaq, Inuit, North America**
The throat singing performed by the Inuits was a form of entertainment. Usually the women would sing duets, competing to see who could last the longest.

▲ **Sean-nós, Ireland**
The melodies of the unaccompanied "old style" Irish songs are often ornamental and sung in the traditional Gaelic language.

▶ **Bull-roarer, Aboriginal, Australia** Since prehistoric times, bull-roarers have been used as ancient musical instruments and for communicating over vast distances by tribes in all continents. They make a roaring sound as they are swung round and round.

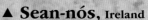

This shaman's rattle is shaped like a raven with the figure of a shaman on its back.

▶ **Montana grass dance, Navajo, North America** Draped in flowing ceremonial dress, the dancer sings dramatically, tensing his throat and vocal chords.

Ancient **world music**

Although very little written music exists from ancient times, historians know about the music from other sources, such as **paintings** on tomb walls, designs on pottery, and the discovery of instruments. Music was important not only for entertainment, but also for religious rituals and **social celebrations**.

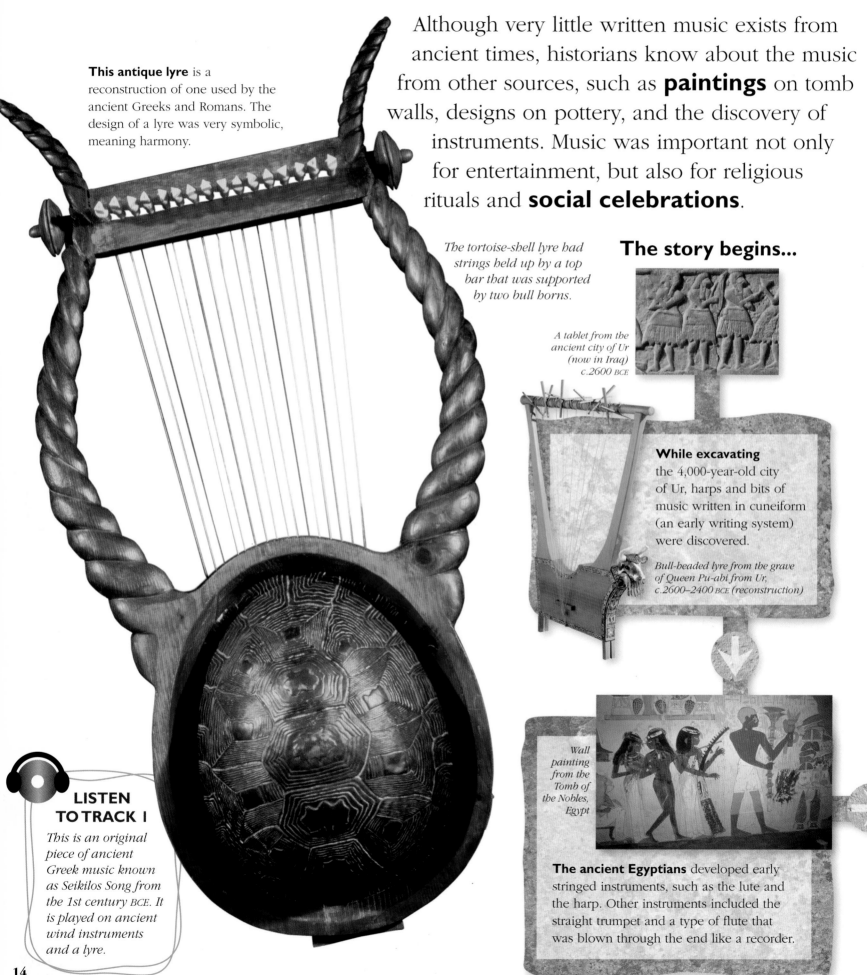

This antique lyre is a reconstruction of one used by the ancient Greeks and Romans. The design of a lyre was very symbolic, meaning harmony.

The tortoise-shell lyre had strings held up by a top bar that was supported by two bull horns.

The story begins...

A tablet from the ancient city of Ur (now in Iraq) c.2600 BCE

While excavating the 4,000-year-old city of Ur, harps and bits of music written in cuneiform (an early writing system) were discovered.

Bull-headed lyre from the grave of Queen Pu-abi from Ur, c.2600–2400 BCE (reconstruction)

Wall painting from the Tomb of the Nobles, Egypt

The ancient Egyptians developed early stringed instruments, such as the lute and the harp. Other instruments included the straight trumpet and a type of flute that was blown through the end like a recorder.

LISTEN TO TRACK 1

This is an original piece of ancient Greek music known as Seikilos Song from the 1st century BCE. It is played on ancient wind instruments and a lyre.

The Romans developed the first brass instruments, making the cornu (the Latin word for horn) from bronze rather than animal horn, for festivals and military use.

Bagpipes originated in ancient times.

The bagpipe was also a popular wind instrument played in countries across the ancient world. It was probably first made by herdsmen using a goat or sheep skin for the bag and a couple of reed pipes.

A Roman mosaic shows a hydraulis – an early organ.

The first keyboard instrument was a hydraulis invented by Ctesibius of Alexandria in 246 BCE. By pressing a note on a board, air pressure was sent into a set of large pipes from a wind chest powered by water and air.

Pupils at the Athenian school in ancient Greece studied music. They were taught to play the aulos (double reed pipe), the kithara (large lyre), and the syrinx (pan-pipes).

The word for music comes from the Greek word *mousike* meaning "art of the Muses". In myths, the nine Muses (spirits) gave the gifts of music, dancing, and singing to humans. The recital of poetry, when read to a lyre accompaniment, became known as a **lyric**.

Music experiments

Historians say the mathematician Pythagorus (c.570–495 BCE) used a monochord (a single-stringed instrument) to explain his theory about the relationship between notes in an **octave scale**.

The Delphic hymn tablet shows words marked with notation – a system of symbols to represent music.

The ancient Greeks worked out music theory, defining music as **tones**, **melody** as the horizontal line of music, and **harmony** as a vertical line of music. They also found a way of writing music down, using a system of signs for each tone.

Bronze bell c.1766–1045 BCE

Ancient Hindu scriptures, the Vedas, mention both Indian classical music (marga) and the veena, a stringed instrument made from gourds (considered the first hollow instrument), in about 600 BCE.

Sarasvati, the goddess of the arts and learning, is often shown playing the veena.

The "Garden Party" relief from the palace of the Assyrian king Ashurbanipal, Nineveh, c.645 BCE

Early Chinese music was played with bronze bells, tuneful stone slabs, and pottery flutes. Confucius, an ancient Chinese philosopher (551–479 BCE), chose music as the symbol of harmony people should strive for.

The oldest known written music, found in Ugarit, Syria, has words and instructions on the tuning of the lyre.

Hymn to Nikkal, the moon goddess, c.1400 BCE

When the Assyrians captured the city of Nineveh, the lives of the talented Hebrew musicians were saved. According to the Bible, the Hebrews sang and used various musical instruments in their worship, such as the shofar, which was made out of a ram or antelope's horn.

Didgeridoo

"The didgeridoo captures the raw resonance of the Australian outback through its deep tones."
William Barton

The didgeridoo is a long tube made from the wood of a hollowed-out **eucalyptus** branch. When a suitable branch is found, it is cut to size, the bark is removed, and a ring of smooth wax or resin is applied around the mouthpiece. The finished didgeridoo may be left plain, or **decorated** with paint, burn marks, or carvings.

Didgeridoos in history

Based on evidence from cave drawings, the didgeridoo originated in Northern Australia over 2,000 years ago.

According to Aboriginal legend, the first didgeridoo was discovered by a man called Burbuk Boon. One cold night, as he was warming himself by the fire, Burbuk Boon picked up a log to add to the flames. The log was very light and Burbuk Boon realized that it had been hollowed out by termites. Burbuk Boon didn't want to throw the termites into the fire so he blew through it, making a great sound. The termites flew out to become the stars in the night sky.

Health benefits
Playing the didgeridoo can improve breathing, reduce snoring, and help people to sleep better at night.

Didgeridoo range
Over three octaves

Playing the didgeridoo

Playing a didgeridoo is a bit like playing a tuba or a trombone. Players place their lips against the wax seal and vibrate them as they blow down the long tube to produce a **low-pitched drone**. They puff out their cheeks and store air in their mouth, breathing through their nose. Players can add other noises as they play, **mimicking** the sounds of animals.

Didgeridoos may be decorated with intricate patterns, important symbols, or scenes from sacred Dreamtime stories.

Other instruments:

Clapsticks
Clapsticks are pairs of sticks about 20 cm (8 in) long, which are **clapped** together to make a noise. They are played with the didgeridoo, or used to beat time for songs and dances.

Bull-roarer
The bull-roarer is a flat, leaf-shaped piece of wood, which is attached to a cord and **whirled** in the air to produce a low-pitched roar.

Top players

In recent years, Aboriginal musicians have brought the didgeridoo to a much wider audience. The band **Yothu Yindi** found fame with their fusion of traditional Aboriginal instruments and Western rock-and-roll. Didgeridoo master **Mark Atkins** has worked with musicians all over the world, including rock guitarist **Jimmy Page** and classical composer **Philip Glass**. Another famous player who likes to mix musical styles is **William Barton**. He can play the didgeridoo and electric guitar at the same time.

Mark Atkins

Most didgeridoos are around 1.2–1.5 m (4–5 ft) long but they can be up to 3 m (10 ft). The longer the didgeridoo, the deeper the sound it produces.

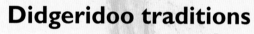

Aborigines playing the clapsticks and didgeridoo

Didgeridoo traditions

The didgeridoo is traditionally used to accompany songs, dances, and sacred Aboriginal **rituals**. Some Aboriginal tribes believe that the didgeridoo should only be played by men. It can be frowned on, or even **forbidden**, for women to play or touch the instrument.

LISTEN TO TRACK 2

Find two sticks or wooden spoons and join in the tapping rhythm of the clapsticks accompanying this piece of didgeridoo music.

Seed rattle

Australian Aborigines may use rattles and shakers to accompany their singing and dancing. These are usually made from the dried seeds of plants and trees such as the boab.

Drum

Some Aboriginal tribes use drums made from the hollowed-out logs of eucalyptus trees. The drum skin is made from the skin of lizards, snakes, or kangaroos.

Gumleaf

The gumleaf is a very simple instrument, made from a single **eucalyptus** leaf. To play the gumleaf, you hold it against your lips and blow. Aborigines originally used the gumleaf to imitate bird noises.

Gumleaf musician Herb Patten

World of wind

From prehistoric flutes and whistles made out of animal bones or hollow plants, an amazing variety of wind instruments has developed. Known as **aerophones**, they are played by blowing into or across holes in a tube, or on a single or double reed attached to a mouthpiece. The **pitch** of the note is fixed by the length of the tube and the number of open holes.

How to blow?

Harmonica – When air is blown and sucked across the holes, the reed plates inside freely vibrate, causing the air inside to vibrate and make the sound.

Clarinet – A single reed of cane is inserted into a metal holder on the mouthpiece. The player's mouth overlaps the reed to make it vibrate, causing the air inside the tube to make sound.

◄ Nose flute,
Prehistoric, Polynesia People from the islands in the Pacific believe that the breath from the nose is purer than the mouth, which can say many hurtful things. The nose flute was used to accompany songs and chants.

▼ Harmonica, 19th century,
Europe Often used in blues (see page 92), American folk music, and jazz, the harmonica, or mouth organ, has free-vibrating metal reeds inside.

► Sheng, pre-500 BCE,
China This bamboo pipe mouth organ is one of the first known free-vibrating reed instruments. Shaped to look like the mythical phoenix, its sound is supposed to imitate the cry of this bird.

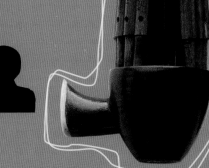

► Accordion, 19th century,
Austria Used in folk music, the sound of this hand-held free reed instrument is produced by steel reeds, which vibrate when air is forced through them by a set of bellows.

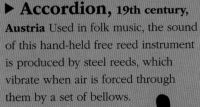

◀ **Zummara, c. 2700 BCE, Egypt** This "double clarinet" has two parallel pipes joined together, each with its own single reed. The player's fingers can cover two holes at a time, one on each pipe.

▶ **Surnai, pre-13th century, Mongolia** This loud folk oboe, with seven holes and a thumb hole on the back, is light and portable, and so is popular with nomadic people. It is played at celebrations such as weddings.

▶ **Flageolet, 16th century, France** Flageolets with single or double pipes (shown) were popular to accompany dances in the 17th and 18th centuries. Played with both hands, they make a bird-like sound.

◀ **Shawm, late 13th century, Europe** This medieval musical instrument was made from a single piece of wood and came in several different sizes. The modern oboe was developed from the shawm.

◀ **Bassoon, c. 1800s, Germany** The largest instrument of the woodwind family with the lowest pitch, the bassoon uses a double reed made from two pieces of cane tied together.

▶ **Pan-pipes, prehistoric, South America** Still played today, pan-pipes have up to three rows of varying-length bamboo strips woven together. The music of the pan-pipes is known as sikuri.

LISTEN TO TRACK 3

The pan-pipes are often associated with South American music. Imagine the sound soaring over the Andes mountains rather like the Andean condor, a large, high-flying bird.

Sounds of **Africa**

Across Africa, different tribes have created their own sounds and instruments. They have their own **music traditions** for ceremonies and village celebrations, which often involve audience participation. However, the main feature of African music is the interweaving of different **rhythmic patterns** known as polyrhythms.

All over Africa
Across the African continent, folk hero Queen Marimba is said to have brought music to the people and to have created many of the instruments still played in Africa today.

A traditional Berber band performing at the Ksour Festival, an international festival of the desert, held in Tunisia each year.

West African griots

The griots are skilled musicians and storytellers who travel between the villages of western Africa. Griots preserve the history of their tribe in **songs** and stories. They keep a record of ancestors, events, and tribal traditions – an important role in a society where little is written down.

Griots performing with a 21-string harp lute called a kora.

Berber bands of North Africa

The Berbers are the native people of North Africa. Berber music has many regional variations but is generally performed by bands of lively **drummers** supported by musicians playing pipes or stringed instruments. At public festivals, many bands come together to perform.

Kenyan Maasai singing

The Maasai of Kenya and northern Tanzania are traditionally a travelling nomadic people. Instruments are an unnecessary burden to the Maasai, who are famous for their distinctive vocal music. Maasai songs follow a pattern of **call and response**, where the first line is sung by the song leader and the response is chanted back by the chorus. While Maasai men sing songs about bravery and hunting, Maasai women sing about family life and looking after the cattle.

Udu clay drum of Nigeria

Most of the people in the Igbo tribe are farmers. The Igbo's most important crop is a root vegetable called the yam, which forms the main staple of their diet. Every year, the Igbo celebrate the yam harvest with a big festival of parades, dances, and music. The Igbo use lots of percussion instruments, such as the **udu clay drum**. Udu drums are traditionally made by women, and played with a combination of hand slapping and finger tapping.

The udu also has a practical use – it doubles as a jug or a storage vessel.

A drum-maker in the village of the royal drum-makers in Buganda.

Timbila of southern Mozambique

The Chopi tribe plays a range of instruments but is famous for its broad-keyed wooden xylophones called **timbilas**. Timbila bands are led by one performer, who improvises the melody, and is followed by the other members of the group. They play music with an elaborate, syncopated (off-beat) rhythm that encourages dancers to move around energetically.

Ngoma drums of Buganda

Ngoma drums are musical instruments used by the Bantu peoples of central, eastern, and southern Africa. The name is applied to different types of drums in different regions. In the Ugandan Kingdom of Buganda, each clan has their own unique drum beat. The **ngoma drums** are a symbol of great power and the most important drums belong to the king.

Bow harps of East Africa

The **bow harp** is a stringed instrument with a curved bow of wood extending out from a hollow resonator. It sits across the lap of the player, who plucks the strings with one hand and damps (stops) the unused strings with the other. The instrument originated in the ancient civilizations of Egypt and Sumer (now Iraq). Over many thousands of years, the use of the bow harp gradually spread southwards. Today, the bow harp is found across Africa and is used by many of the tribal groups of Uganda and Sudan.

Sudanese bow harp with a gourd (dried fruit) resonator.

LISTEN TO TRACK 4

Listen for the call-and-response pattern in this traditional ceremonial song sung by Kenyan Maasai women.

Mbira of Zimbabwe

The music of the Shona tribe often involves a small thumb piano known as the **mbira**. Laid out on a small wooden board, the mbira has staggered metal keys. At religious ceremonies the mbira player is accompanied by another musician with a rattle.

Plucky **pipa**

"The thicker strings rattled like splatters of sudden rain, the thinner ones hummed like a hushed whisper." Bai Juyi – Tang Dynasty poet

A woman playing the pipa is shown on a Qing dynasty porcelain vase.

Chinese instruments

Chinese orchestras traditionally consist of bowed strings, plucked strings, woodwinds, and percussion. However, individual Chinese instruments are divided into eight sounds made from eight different materials. These are silk, bamboo, wood, stone, metal, clay, gourd (dried fruit), and hide.

SILK INSTRUMENTS *use twisted silk for strings and includes Chinese versions of harps, fiddles, lutes, and zithers.*

BAMBOO INSTRUMENTS *are woodwind instruments like Chinese versions of flutes, oboes, and reed pipes.*

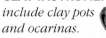

WOOD INSTRUMENTS *are mostly very ancient percussion instruments such as woodblocks hit with sticks.*

STONE INSTRUMENTS *are mostly stone chimes.*

METAL INSTRUMENTS *include bells, cymbals, and gongs.*

CLAY INSTRUMENTS *include clay pots and ocarinas.*

GOURD INSTRUMENTS *include reed mouth organs.*

HIDE INSTRUMENTS *are drums.*

The pipa is a four-stringed pear-shaped instrument that looks like a lute. It is one of the world's oldest instruments **(over 2,000 years old)** and also one of the most popular. The pipa is played all over China.

A pipa player needs extremely nimble fingers to play well. The instrument is held pointing upwards and the **left hand** moves up and down the frets, pushing, twisting, and pulling the strings. The player's five fingers on the **right hand** alternate between plucking the strings forwards and backwards.

A girl learns to pluck.

This pipa sheet music is written in Chinese characters.

Stemknoppen

Kop

Top pipa player

Liu Fang is a famous pipa player and travels the world performing solo concerts. She started playing at the age of six and was quickly recognized to be a child prodigy, giving public concerts by the age of nine, and playing for Queen Elizabeth II at age 11. Liu Fang plays Western classical music, as well as traditional Chinese music, on her pipa and also combines the two musical traditions.

Liu Fang (1974–) performing at Womad, UK, on 25 July, 2004.

A pipa typically has four strings.

Woman in traditional costume playing the pipa

*Its short, bent neck has up to **30 frets,** which extend onto the soundboard, offering a wide range (3½ octaves).*

Fake nails

Up until the 20th century, players used their **fingernails** to pluck soft, twisted strings made of silk. Now, however, the strings are made of steel with nylon wound around them and are too strong for human fingernails. Instead false nails are used, made from **plastic or tortoise-shell**, and fixed to the player's fingertips with elastic tape.

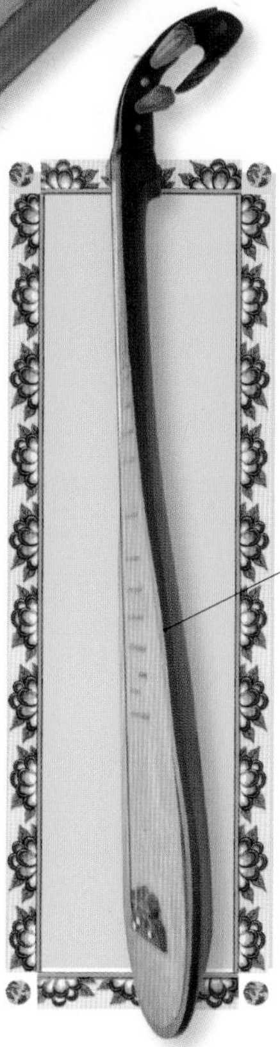

The pipa is a very narrow instrument, as you can see from this side view.

A man uses false fingernails to play.

23

Things with strings

Since ancient times, stringed instruments, known as **chordophones**, have developed in all shapes and sizes. These instruments make sounds by vibrating strings. The strings may be played with a bow, plucked with fingers, or struck with hammers. Nearly all chordophones are made up of strings stretched across a **resonator** – the hollow part of the instrument that vibrates along with the strings, making them sound more musical.

The five basic types of chordophones

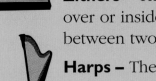 **Lutes** – The strings are stretched over a resonator and along a neck, as in guitars and violins.

Zithers – The strings are stretched over or inside a resonator, or between two resonators.

Harps – The strings are slanted within a frame.

Lyres – The strings are raised on a bar above the resonator.

Musical bows – The strings are stretched from one end of a bow to the other.

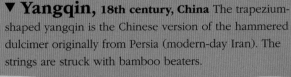

▼ **Yangqin,** 18th century, **China** The trapezium-shaped yangqin is the Chinese version of the hammered dulcimer originally from Persia (modern-day Iran). The strings are struck with bamboo beaters.

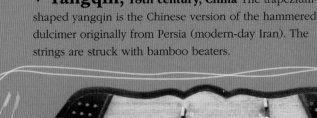

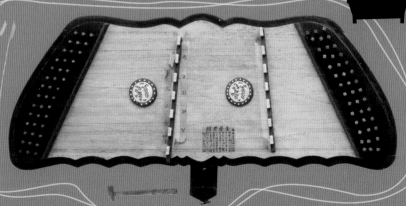

 ▲ **Medieval lute,** c. 1350–1400, **Europe** Lutes were very popular, accompanying songs in medieval Europe, and continued to be heard during the Renaissance and Baroque periods (see page 38). They have rarely been used since the early 1800s.

 ◄ **Balalaika,** 18th century, **Russia** This Russian folk instrument has a characteristic triangular body and three strings. There are at least six sizes of balalaika varying from low to high pitch.

LISTEN TO TRACK 5

Try humming along to this traditional Chinese melody played on the erhu, accompanied by the Chinese zither and harp. Chinese music uses a five note (pentatonic) scale.

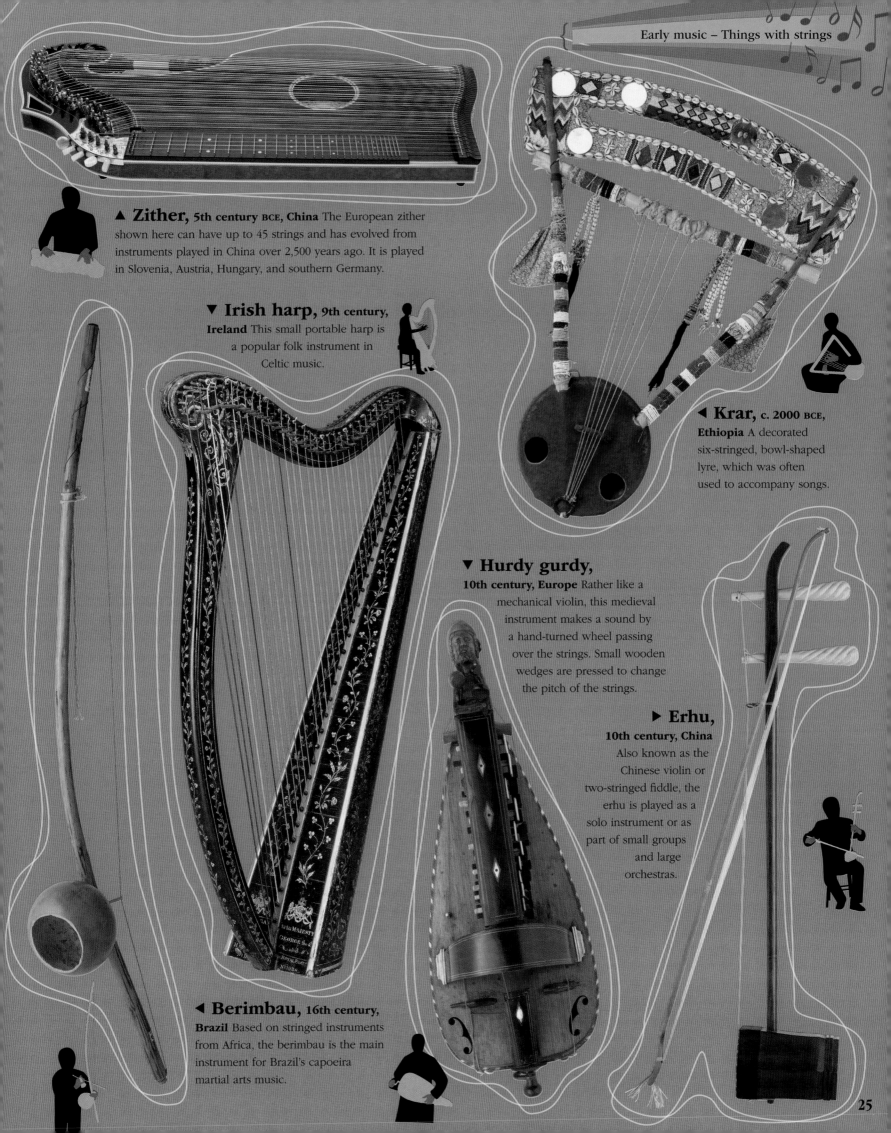

▲ **Zither,** 5th century BCE, **China** The European zither shown here can have up to 45 strings and has evolved from instruments played in China over 2,500 years ago. It is played in Slovenia, Austria, Hungary, and southern Germany.

▼ **Irish harp,** 9th century, **Ireland** This small portable harp is a popular folk instrument in Celtic music.

◀ **Krar,** c. 2000 BCE, **Ethiopia** A decorated six-stringed, bowl-shaped lyre, which was often used to accompany songs.

▼ **Hurdy gurdy,** 10th century, **Europe** Rather like a mechanical violin, this medieval instrument makes a sound by a hand-turned wheel passing over the strings. Small wooden wedges are pressed to change the pitch of the strings.

▶ **Erhu,** 10th century, **China** Also known as the Chinese violin or two-stringed fiddle, the erhu is played as a solo instrument or as part of small groups and large orchestras.

◀ **Berimbau,** 16th century, **Brazil** Based on stringed instruments from Africa, the berimbau is the main instrument for Brazil's capoeira martial arts music.

Ziryab (Blackbird)

Musician's biography
Ali Ibn Nafi (**Ziryab**)

Details of Ziryab's life and dates are debated amongst historians.

c. 789: *Born possibly in Tanzania, and later taken to Baghdad as a slave, or born in Baghdad. From an early age, he was trained in music by the musician Ishaq al-Mawsili.*

c. 813: *Left Baghdad and travelled to Islamic courts in Sham, Syria, and then to Ifriqiyya, in Tunisia.*

822: *In his 30s, he settled in Cordoba, southern Spain, and became the court musician at the royal court of Abd ar-Rahmān II.*

857: *Died in Cordoba.*

LISTEN TO TRACK 6
This is the sound of an oud. Try to tap out the beat of the Middle Eastern oud rhythm.

Persians traded silk, carpets, and ceramics like this 8th-century Persian vase.

Musician's influences

8th-century Baghdad
Baghdad (now the capital of Iraq) was a centre of learning and trade and the largest city of the Persian empire during the Islamic Golden Age of the 8th and 9th centuries.

Ishaq al-Mawsili (767–850)
Ishaq, and his father Ibrahim, were famous and highly skilled Persian court musicians, who had a huge influence in developing classical Arabic music. Ishaq taught Ziryab but became jealous of his pupil's musical talents.

"After the arrival of (Ziryab), a wind of pleasure and luxurious life blew through Cordoba."
Henri Terrasse – French historian, 1958

Ziryab, meaning **blackbird**, was the nickname given to Ali Ibn Nafi, a talented 9th-century Persian court musician with an amazing voice. He grew up and learnt music in Baghdad (now in Iraq), which was a centre of music and culture. However, he was forced to leave because his music teacher was jealous of his extraordinary talents, so he settled at the Islamic court in southern Spain and became a **legend**.

Playing the oud
Like the modern-day musician shown here, Ziryab played the Arabian lute called an oud. This is a pear-shaped, stringed instrument from the Middle East. Historians believe that it was Ziryab who added a fifth pair of strings, dyed a symbolic colour, and began using an eagle's feather to pluck the strings.

Arabic classical music is sung or performed by a solo instrumentalist or singer. It is very rhythmic, and it is described as monophonic, having one line of sound with no harmonies.

Oud player

Ziryab's music influenced wandering minstrels across medieval Europe. These minstrels were travelling entertainers who moved from town to town singing songs of distant places and imaginary events.

A musical legacy

Ziryab set up one of the first colleges of music in Europe, which taught both men and women. This **conservatory** encouraged and developed new and **experimental** sounds and styles of music. Ziryab introduced Middle Eastern instruments, songs, and dances and mixed them with Spanish gypsy music. From this, the oud became the Spanish guitar and the famous **flamenco** dance was created. Historians have also written that all of Ziryab's eight sons and two daughters were great musicians and spread their father's music throughout medieval Europe, influencing the music of travelling and court musicians, known as **minstrels** and troubadours.

Flamenco is a dramatic gypsy-dance style of Andalusia, southern Spain, performed by women wearing colourful flowing dresses, who finger snap or clap the strong rhythm accompanied by mysterious-sounding guitar music.

Celebrity trendsetter

At the royal court of Cordoba, Ziryab was admired for his elegant manners and intelligence. Historians have written that through his celebrity status, he introduced **cultural practices** from the Middle East. Many are still used today.

Food

Ziryab introduced new fruits and vegetables, such as asparagus, and **new recipes** from Baghdad. He established the use of tablecloths and glassware and how they were to be set out on a table. He even insisted on three-course meals with a soup, a main course, and a dessert, which became the **banqueting style** across Europe and is still used in fine-dining restaurants today.

Fashion

Ziryab introduced not only new clothing styles and shorter hairstyles but also the idea of wearing different clothes for each season and at different times of the day. In winter, clothes were to be made from warm cotton or wool and in dark colours, while in summer, clothes were to be made from cool, light materials in bright colours and he introduced bleached white clothing. Fashion shops today continue to have their **seasonal collections**.

Hygiene

Ziryab is also known as the inventor of one of the first pleasant-tasting toothpastes that actually worked. He also introduced a new type of under-arm deodorant. He opened a **beauty parlour** for women, introducing new perfumes and cosmetics, and improved hair conditioner, and introduced shaving for men. Getting ready for a party wouldn't be the same without Ziryab's trendsetting!

Gamelan music

The gamelan is thought of as one instrument played by many people, producing a unique sound.

Ostinato: *Gamelan tunes are made up of a phrase that is repeated over and over. In musical terminology, this repeated phrase is called ostinato. Traditional gamelan musicians learn their parts by ear and memorize them as written music is not used.*

Interlocking: *Each gamelan instrument has its own phrase to play over and over again (ostinato). When all the instruments play their own phrases together, it's called interlocking. This is an important feature of Balinese gamelan music called kotèkan. This is what makes a complete tune.*

Bebranangan: *Bebranangan is a typical Balinese gamelan tune. There are three sections of two notes each. The sections have different rhythms and are played by different parts of the gamelan. When they are played together, the whole song is heard.*

Wayang kulit: *A shadow puppet theatre, or wayang kulit, is a Javanese tradition. The plays, which often tell cultural and religious stories, are performed with a gamelan as accompaniment and often last all night.*

The gamelan

"Gamelan is comparable to only two things, moonlight and flowing water." Jaap Kunst

The gamelan is a traditional **Indonesian orchestra** that performs at ceremonies and celebrations. There are two main types of gamelan, those from **Bali** (shown here) and those from **Java**. Individual gamelans may be made up of different instruments, but most typically have drums, gongs, and metallophones (tuned metal instruments).

Gamelans have been used for centuries as a way of spreading religious messages.

Sacred instrument

A Javanese legend reveals that the first gamelan was formed around **1,800 years ago** by the ruler Sang Hyang Guru, who used a set of gongs to summon the **gods**. A gamelan is sacred: musicians must take their shoes off to play, and no one can step over the instruments.

Playing together

Every musician is equal in the gamelan orchestra. The **drummer** leads (he plays the rhythm that the other musicians follow), but he has no higher **status** than anyone else. Usually men and women play in separate gamelans, apart from when a woman sings with a male gamelan orchestra.

The drummer sets the pace of the music.

Each instrument has its own part to play in gamelan music, from the main theme and rhythm to punchy notes and elaboration.

Gender metallophones *have squared metal bars in a wooden frame. The mallets used on them are covered in felt so they produce a softened sound to elaborate the tune.*

Drums are the main rhythm instrument. There may be three or four different-sized **kendang** *drums in a gamelan. The heads on each drum are different sizes too. A larger head makes a deeper sound than a smaller one.*

Saron metallophones *have rounded metal bars that are struck with a mallet made of wood or horn. They play the main tune.*

Cradled gongs called **bonang** *add chiming sounds to the main theme, either to elaborate or to punctuate.*

LISTEN TO TRACK 7
This is an extract of a gamelan playing. Would you describe the music as like moonlight and flowing water?

The **Gong Ageng** *is said to be the main spirit of this entire Balinese gamelan.*

Rituals and religious music

Around the world, music has been used in religious ceremonies, at tribal gatherings, and for important occasions. Elaborate or simple, music creates the right **atmosphere** for a celebration, honouring royalty, or a spiritual and worshipful experience.

▲ **Gregorian chant,**
c. 6–10th century, Europe This manuscript shows the notation for a Gregorian chant. Named after Pope Gregory I, Gregorian chants were performed by monks throughout Europe, and influenced the direction of all Western music that followed.

LISTEN TO TRACK 8

This begins as a piece of 16th-century plainchant, which is sung in Latin and unaccompanied. How does this differ from the four-part singing of the full choir that follows?

▶ **Akhmatova Requiem, 1980, John Tavener**
The requiem mass is a Roman Catholic service accompanied by music and held in honour of the dead. John Tavener based his Akhmatova Requiem on a Byzantine chant, using the funeral text of the Russian Orthodox Church and the poems of Anna Akhmatova (above).

▲ **Royal Ancestral Rite, 14th century, South Korea** The Jongmyo Shrine is the burial site of the kings and queens of the Chosun dynasty. As part of the ritual ceremonies held at the shrine each year, musicians and dancers perform to entertain the spirits of dead ancestors.

▼ **Soweto Gospel Choir, 2008, South Africa** Celebrating Nelson Mandela's 90th birthday, this South African choir performed gospel music with its catchy rhythms and repeated choruses.

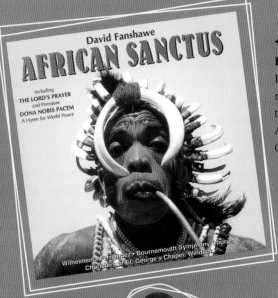

◄ **African Sanctus,** 1972,
David Fanshawe The composer and explorer
David Fanshawe travelled through Africa to
record the traditional music of over 50 African
tribes. In *African Sanctus,* he mixed the tribal
African music with the songs of the Roman
Catholic Church's Latin mass.

► **Missa Gloria tibi Trinitas,**
1526, John Taverner As a master of the
choristers at Cardinal College, Oxford, John
Taverner wrote music to accompany the services
held at the Cathedral. *Missa Gloria tibi Trinitas*
was the first of eight masses he composed.

◄ **Mevlevi dancers,**
13th century, Turkey Also known
as whirling dervishes, these modern
dancers belong to an order of Sufi
Muslims who follow the teachings of
the ancient Persian poet and theologian
Mevlâna Jalâluddîn Rumi. They worship
God through the Sema – a ceremony of
song and dance. The 18th-century
Turkish composer Dede Efendi wrote a
great deal of Mevlevi music.

▼ **National anthems,** 2004, **Athens Olympics**
Each country has a special song that is played at important public events,
such as sports competitions, or the arrival of visiting dignitaries. When
the German women's hockey team won gold at the Athens Olympics in
2004, they sang their national anthem, *Das Deutschlandlied.*

▲ **Maori singers,** 1992, **The Cook Islands**
The Maori use waiata (songs) and karakia (prayers or
incantations) for welcoming, entertainment, prayers, or
to communicate their feelings at tribal events.

31

Indian classical music

The classical music styles in India are divided between north and south.

This 18th-century painting shows an Indian prince and princess listening to music.

HINDUSTANI MUSIC, *the north Indian system, produces music in a freer form and style. The focus is on the solo singer, who improvises to create variations for the melody line (raga), which vary in mood. Traditional accompanying instruments such as the tabla and sitar are now taking a more important role of their own, especially outside South Asia.*

The saraswati veena (see page 15) is a popular stringed instrument in southern India for playing the raga.

CARNATIC MUSIC, *the south Indian system, relies on a rigid musical structure. Vocal music is the main focus, usually accompanied by a small instrumental group, such as violin, tambura, and veena. The singer performs the raga, using semitone notes to give various melody lines. The rhythm (tala) is also important and there are many variations.*

LISTEN TO TRACK 9

This piece of Indian music is played by two sitars, a tambura, and a tabla. Listen for the drone and the tala (rhythm).

Sitar, tabla, and *tambura*

"In our culture we have such respect for musical instruments, they are like part of God."
Ravi Shankar – Indian sitar player

Indian classical music has been passed down from generation to generation for more than 3,000 years. Although the music varies between the north and the south of India, the pieces share the common idea of having three main parts: the raga, a single melody line, accompanied by a constant fixed note called a drone, and the tala, which is the rhythm. The **sitar, tabla,** and **tambura** are an example of a group of instruments that plays these parts.

The tabla is a pair of drums: the right one, often made from wood, is called dayan, and the left one is made out of metal and called bayan. The drumheads are covered with goat or cow hide and different parts make different sounds. The tabla plays the **tala** part – a cycle of beats played throughout the piece.

At the centre of both drumheads is a black spot made of flour and iron filings, which when struck makes a bell-like sound.

Top players

Indian classical music is very complex to play. **Ravi Shankar** received international fame as a sitar player when **George Harrison** of the Beatles (see page 108) became his student in 1966. Shankar's former wife, **Annapurna Devi**, and daughter, **Anoushka**, are also exceptional sitar players. **Alla Rakha** and now his son **Zakir Hussain** are legendary tabla players who both made the instrument more popular.

Ravi Shankar playing the sitar in 1960.

The surpeti

Other Indian drone instruments include the surpeti. This is a small reed-free organ with no keys that has small bellows pumped by hand to produce the drone sound. There is also an electronic version used today.

The sitar is a long-necked string instrument with three sets of strings. One set of four strings provides the melody (**raga**), another set of two or three strings supplies a rhythmic ostinato (**drone**), and the final set of nine or 13 "sympathetic" strings vibrates underneath the other strings, giving the sitar its characteristic **jangling** sound.

A player sits with the base of the sitar balanced between the left foot and the right knee.

The tambura (also known as tanpura) can only play the **drone** part as it has four long strings, which are plucked one after another. The drone gives the piece of music an atmosphere and sets the mode, or scale, of the raga.

33

Kengyo is a title given to highly talented blind musicians. Before the 20th century, most music in Japan was played by blind musicians, who were monks.

Yatsuhashi Kengyo

Musician's biography

Yatsuhashi **Kengyo**

1614: *Yatsuhashi was born.*

c.1630: *Taught to play koto by Buddhist priest Kenjun.*

1685: *He died aged 71.*

Yatsuhashi sweets
Yatsuhashi is a cinnamon-flavoured sweet from Kyoto, Japan, that is shaped like a koto and named after the composer.

Playing the koto
Koto players wear three ivory picks on their right hand: one on their thumb and the others on the first two fingers. They use these to pluck the strings.

The very talented blind Japanese musician, Yatsuhashi Kengyo, is known as the **"father of modern koto"**. Before the 17th century, the koto (a Japanese stringed instrument) was only played with other instruments in the royal court and temples. Yatsuhashi developed new **techniques** for playing the koto and composed many solo pieces. His works increased the popularity of the koto as an instrument everyone could play, and its appeal continues today.

Koto players kneel and lean forward to pluck the strings a little away from the right end.

Music stand

Bridge

Rokudan no Shirabe
(Study in Six Steps), 17th century

Rokudan no Shirabe
Yatsuhashi's best-known composition *Rokudan no Shirabe* (*Study in Six Steps*) contains all the **basic techniques** musicians need for playing the koto, and is the most played classical koto piece of music. Each dan (or step) has 52 beats and the piece has **six variations** that begin slowly and get faster. Other composers have since adapted its melody, written it for other instruments, and added additional instrumental parts.

The koto is the national instrument of Japan.

An 18th century sankyoku ensemble

Sankyoku ensemble

Along with the koto, the shamisen (a three-stringed banjo-like instrument) and the kokyu (a three-stringed instrument played with a bow) also became popular during the 17th century. These instruments were played together in a group called **sankyoku**, meaning three instrument ensemble. The players also sang as they played.

The shape of the **koto** is said to resemble a dragon, and the player kneels near the right end of the instrument – the "head" of the dragon.

The **kokyu** is slightly smaller than the shamisen and is played with a bow. The hollow body was made from coconut or japonica wood.

The three strings of the **shamisen** were plucked using a plectrum (a small flat tool) called a bachi.

Since the 19th century, the **shakuhachi** (a bamboo flute) has replaced the kokyu.

Shakuhachi

Tuning a koto

Under each of the 13 strings is a **moveable bridge**, which raises the string above the body of the koto, allowing it to vibrate when plucked. The strings are tuned depending on where the bridges are positioned, and the bridges can be raised or lowered during a piece of music, changing the tuning of the strings. This makes the koto both challenging to play and **flexible** for playing many different styles of music.

Classical **music**
(1600–1900)

Since the 1600s, famous composers have given **Western music** particular structures and styles. Their music is still enjoyed and performed all over the world today.

Baroque (1600–1750)

The Baroque era was a period of great developments in European music – the birth of opera, the growth of the orchestra, and an increase in instrumental music. The style gradually broke away from the complex interweaving music of Medieval and Renaissance music and vocal music became more **dramatic**.

The story starts here...

The Concert in the Egg *painted in the 15th century by Hieronymus Bosch.*

Between the 12th and 16th centuries, composers developed polyphonic music – continuous, flowing pieces of **interweaving** melody lines sung by different voice parts. Greatly admired composers included Léonin, Pérotin, Guillaume Dufay, Josquin des Prez, Giovanni Palestrina, and Orlande de Lassus.

Around 1030, an Italian monk, Guido d'Arezzo, created the music stave to give notes a definite pitch. He designed a system of four lines and placed notes on the lines and in the spaces. Musicians could now read and write music.

Music STAVE

Between the 6th and 11th centuries, medieval church music moved on from plainchant (voices singing a single melody line) to introducing a number of **voice parts** from treble to bass. The parts imitated the sound of the organ, which played widely spaced chords.

VOCAL music

From the mid-15th century, great cultural changes were taking place across Europe in a period known as the **Renaissance**. Tradesmen, such as the German Meistersingers, began performing music, wealthy families paid for vocal and instrumental music, and music could now be printed and sold everywhere.

15th century nuns singing

Polyphony became a key feature of **sacred music**. The plainchant was merged with more vocal lines, each with different words, to create a piece called a motet. Catholic composers like Giovanni Gabrieli wrote elaborate masses as musical settings of the services, while Protestant composers like Thomas Tallis wrote repetitive, less complex anthems.

CHORAL sacred music

Family singing a madrigal

Madrigals were popular non-religious songs for several unaccompanied voices. Composers, such as the Italian Luca Marenzio and the English Thomas Weelkes, used a technique called **word painting** – music imitating the meaning of the words.

MADRIGALS

Viol

Many **instruments** originated during the Renaissance, such as viols, sackbuts, and recorders, while other existing ones were improved. The virginal and harpsichord were popular **keyboard** instruments.

At the start of the 17th century, the Italian Monteverdi influenced a new musical style, Baroque. His drama music, later known as opera, used **monody** – one vocal part accompanied by an instrument playing chords underneath, known as the **basso continuo**.

Claudio MONTEVERDI (1567–1643)

Baroque composers developed many new forms of music...

Vocal music

Barbara Strozzi (1619–1677)

This Venetian female singer composed more non-religious choral music than any other Baroque composer. Strozzi's music developed the **cantata** – a dramatic vocal piece.

Jean-Baptiste Lully (1632–1687)

An influential composer of the French court, Lully wrote grand operas, ballets, and **theatrical music**. He died from gangrene after stabbing his toe with a cane that he conducted with.

Henry Purcell (1659–1695)

English composer Purcell included Italian and French musical styles in his music. *Dido and Aeneas*, first performed in 1689, was the first full-length **English opera**.

Johann Pachelbel (1653–1706)

This German court organist is known for his keyboard and chamber music. He developed **canons** and **fugues**, where a single melody is repeated at different times by different parts.

Arcangelo Corelli (1653–1713)

Corelli was an influential composer and a superb violinist. He developed new playing techniques shown in his **trio sonatas** – pieces for two solo instruments and a basso continuo.

François Couperin (1668–1733)

A French organist and harpsichordist, Couperin gave a weekly concert, often playing **suites** – a collection of dances for one or more instruments.

Instrumental music

George Frideric Handel (1685–1759)

German-born, Handel moved to England where he wrote 40 operas, 20 **oratorios** (see page 42), and many other vocal and instrumental pieces including *Water Music* (1717), which is three suites, each in different keys.

George Philipp Telemann (1681–1767)

This famous German instrumental composer wrote a huge number of concertos for unusual combinations of instruments. He **experimented** with the combination of sounds produced by both old and new instruments.

Antonio Vivaldi (1678–1741)

A violin virtuoso, Vivaldi is best known for composing *The Four Seasons*. This work helped to develop the **concerto** – a piece in three sections for a solo instrument and accompanying orchestra.

Musician's biography
Johann Sebastian **Bach**

1685: *Bach was born in Eisenach, Germany, into a musical family. His father was the town musician. He was the youngest of eight children.*

1695: *Aged 10, Bach moved in with his older brother who was an organist. His brother probably taught Bach the organ.*

1703: *Aged 18, he became a low-level court musician, playing the violin and organ.*

1707: *Bach married his cousin, Maria. They had seven children together.*

1717: *Aged 32, Bach became chapel master in the court of Prince Leopold of Anhalt-Cohen.*

1721: *Bach married Anna Wilcke, as his first wife had died in 1720. He had another 13 children.*

1723: *Aged 38, he moved to Leipzig where he became a teacher and director in St Thomas's Church.*

1729: *Became Director of Collegium Musicum of Leipzig, performing concerts in a local coffee house.*

1750: *Aged 65, Bach was left blind and ill after two eye operations. He died of a stroke and was buried at St Thomas's Church.*

Musician's influences

Girolamo Frescobaldi (1583–1643)
Italian composer whose collection of organ music was studied by many Baroque musicians.

Johann Pachelbel (1653–1706)
German composer and organ teacher, Pachelbel taught Bach's elder brother Johann Christoph and also developed organ music.

Johann Sebastian Bach

"All one has to do is hit the right keys at the right time and the instrument plays itself."

During Johann Sebastian Bach's lifetime, people merely thought of him as an **ordinary** working musician. No one really knew much about his music. However, in 1829 (79 years after his death), another composer, Felix Mendelssohn, conducted a performance of his *St Matthew's Passion* to great acclaim. Bach was back!

Bach was not only a prolific composer, but he also found time to father 20 children. He called five of them Johann, and two Johanna, and four of his sons became famous musicians and composers themselves. His family was so large and musical that the word for musician in one area of Germany was "Bach".

LISTEN TO TRACK 10
This organ piece is a prelude by J. S. Bach. An organ may have more than one keyboard played by the hands and a pedalboard played by the feet. Before and during the piece, an organ player can turn on and off the stops to allow air only to pass through certain pipes.

The organ at St Thomas's Church in Leipzig, Germany, where Bach played and composed much of his work.

These handwritten notes by Bach are thought to be one of the earliest of his writings, dated around 1700. The notes were discovered in the Duchess Anna Amalia Library in Weimar, Germany.

Organ maestro

Bach is now seen as one of the greatest geniuses in music history. He wrote all kinds of music – for orchestras and choirs, as well as **concertos** for many different instrumental combinations. But perhaps he is best known for his **organ music**, such as *Toccata and Fugue in D minor*. Ironically, Bach never had his own organ and played on many different ones. His compositions range from very simple to very difficult.

Gould is also known for his eccentric style of playing. He sat very low over the piano, swaying in a clockwise direction and humming along to the music.

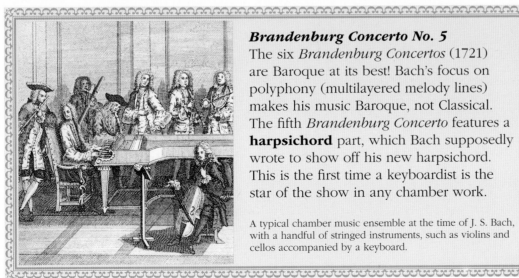

Brandenburg Concerto No. 5
The six *Brandenburg Concertos* (1721) are Baroque at its best! Bach's focus on polyphony (multilayered melody lines) makes his music Baroque, not Classical. The fifth *Brandenburg Concerto* features a **harpsichord** part, which Bach supposedly wrote to show off his new harpsichord. This is the first time a keyboardist is the star of the show in any chamber work.

A typical chamber music ensemble at the time of J. S. Bach, with a handful of stringed instruments, such as violins and cellos accompanied by a keyboard.

Glenn Gould (1932–1982)

When some people think of Bach, they also think of the Canadian pianist Glenn Gould. Gould's **recordings** of Bach's *Goldberg Variations* (1741) have won him Grammys and worldwide acclaim. A 'variation' is a piece of music where the theme is repeated with changes – to the harmony, rhythm, or instruments used.

Grand oratorios

An oratorio tells a **story in music** and is performed by solo singers, a choir, and an orchestra. Although similar to opera, oratorios are generally not performed with scenery or costumes. At first, the stories were religious ones taken from the Bible, but now composers also look to literature and historical events for their inspiration.

▲ **The Creation**, 1798, **Franz Joseph Haydn** Haydn uses music to tell the story of the creation; from the emptiness of space to the teeming life of the Garden of Eden. Soloists sing the parts of the Archangels and the first humans, Adam and Eve.

▲ **Belshazzar's Feast**, 1931, **William Walton** Belshazzar, the King of Babylon, has enslaved the Jewish people and looted their temples. At a great feast, Belshazzar and his nobles get drunk on wine and praise the "gods" of gold and silver. The disembodied hand of God appears and warns arrogant Belshazzar that he will be slain.

LISTEN TO TRACK 11

This is part of the Hallelujah chorus from Messiah *by Handel, performed by a Baroque orchestra and full choir.*

◄ **Messiah**, 1741, **George Frideric Handel**
Handel's oratorio tells of the Old Testament prophesies about the *Messiah*, or "King of the Jews". It follows the life of Jesus Christ from his birth and the miracles he performed, to his crucifixion, death, and resurrection. Shown here is a modern interpretation by the English National Opera.

▲ The Death of Captain Cook, 1978, Anne Boyd

Captain James Cook was the first explorer to chart the coastlines of Australia and New Zealand, and to discover the islands of Hawaii. This oratorio of Australian composer Anne Boyd tells of Cook's death at the hands of the Hawaiian natives after arguing about a stolen boat.

▲ Carmina Burana, 1936, Carl Orff

Based on a collection of medieval poems about morals, love, luck, drinking, gambling, and the arrival of spring, Orff's original idea was as a piece for the stage. *Carmina Burana* is now mainly performed as a large-scale choral work, and has become one of the most popular and recognizable modern oratorios. Full of dramatic chanting and booming percussion, the work continues to be very theatrical.

▲ A Child of Our Time, 1941, Michael Tippett

Inspired by events at the start of World War II, *A Child of Our Time* tells the story of a young Jewish refugee who shot a German embassy official in Paris in 1938, triggering riots in Nazi Germany and the start of a campaign of violence against the Jews.

▲ St. Luke's Passion, 1966, Krzysztof Penderecki

Many musical works have been inspired by the death of Christ. This avant-garde oratorio is almost all atonal and has three choruses and a boy's choir that shout, giggle, hiss, groan, and whistle through the performance, and an organ and brass section that often play very loud chords called tone clusters, using notes close together.

▲ A Dylan Thomas Trilogy, 1976 (revised 1999), John Corigliano

The result of a life-long interest and 50 years of work, John Corigliano's "memory play" in the form of an oratorio is built around the poems of Dylan Thomas.

▲ Nâzim, 2001, Fazil Say

This oratorio depicts the life and works of the Turkish revolutionary poet Nâzim Hikmet. *Nâzim* is performed by an orchestra of more than 200 musicians.

Violins in history

Ancient, Central Asia:

Ancient two-stringed instruments played with horse-hair bows, such as the kobyz from Kazakhstan and the kyl kyyak from Kyrgyzstan, were probably forerunners of the Arabic rabab. In Central Asia, horse-riders would play while riding.

Late 800s, Middle East: *The Arabic rabab had two silk strings attached to a pear-shaped gourd (dried fruit) with a long neck. It was played on the lap or on the floor with a bow.*

1000s, Europe: *The rebec in Spain was a variation on the rabab. It usually had five strings and a wooden body and was placed on the shoulder.*

1200s: *The vielle in France had five strings, and looked more like a modern violin, but with a C-shaped hole.*

1500s: *The viola di braccio in Italy looked like the vielle but only had 3 strings. It had a f-shaped hole like the modern violin.*

1555: *Andrea Amati, considered the father of the modern violin, created the first four-string violin.*

1644–1737: *Antonio Stradivari, an apprentice of Amati's grandson Nicolo, made world-famous violins.*

1600s–1700s: *Venice, Cremona, and Brescia in Italy and Innsbruck in Austria became important violin-making centres.*

1600s: *During the Baroque period, the violin started to be included regularly in orchestras and for chamber music.*

Violin range

Four octaves

Vivacious **violin**

"A table, a chair, a bowl of fruit and a violin; what else does a man need to be happy." Albert Einstein – physicist and accomplished violinist

The violin is the smallest and highest pitched of the instruments in the **string family**, which includes the viola, cello, and double bass. Violins have been traditionally used as an accompaniment to singing and dancing.

The violin is held under the chin with the bow in the right hand. The bow is drawn across the strings at right angles while the left hand's fingers press the strings on the neck.

Chin rest

Bridge

F-holes

Tailpiece button

Tailpiece

Frog

Screw

Electrifying!

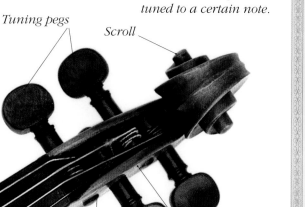

Electric violins have been used since the 1920s. Some are not made from wood, but built with **lightweight** materials, such as kevlar and glass.

Violin strings are tuned by turning the relevant pegs. Each string is tuned to a certain note.

Tuning pegs

Scroll

Strings

Traditionally, strings were made from animal gut, but they tend to snap quite easily. Nowadays, metal strings are used.

Fingerboard

Pegbox

Nut (a small second bridge)

Neck

Hair

Bow hair is either horse hair or synthetic.

Bow

LISTEN TO TRACK 12

A solo violin is the main instrument in this piece called "Spring" from The Four Seasons *composed by Antonio Vivaldi in 1723 (see page 39).*

Bows should be rubbed regularly with rosin. This helps the bow strings grip the violin strings, making them vibrate. Rosin is the resin, or sap, of conifers, such as pine. It is made by heating up liquid resin to purify it, and then cooling it.

Priceless violins

The Italian craftsman, **Antonio Stradivari** (1644–1737), is still considered to be the most famous violin maker of all time. He worked out the best thickness of the wood, changed the scroll, and used a brighter varnish. Many violin makers have since copied his designs. In 2006, the Stradivarius "Hammer" was sold for over US$3.5 million to an anonymous bidder – the highest price ever paid for an instrument in an auction.

The Stradivarius "Solomon", made in 1729, sold for US$2.728 million on 2 April, 2007.

Top violinists

Classical composers have challenged violinists to develop many intricate skills to play their compositions. But since childhood, some players have achieved impressive abilities. Famous child prodigies include **Niccolò Paganini** and **Joseph Joachim** and, since the 20th century, **Jascha Heiftz, Yehudi Menuhin, Bin Huang, Midori,** and **Maxim Vengerov**. **Sarah Chang** (left) started playing when she was aged four and was captivating audiences in concerts around the world by age eight. She recorded her first album aged 10. Violinists have made their mark on popular music as well.

Damien and Tourie Escobar, known as the group "Nuttin But Stringz", play hip hop violin music.

Classical (1750–1820)

The story continues...

By the mid-18th century, the classical music forms, such as sonatas, concertos, and oratorios, had become established. The composers of the Classical era aimed to create music that was **elegant** and **perfect**. The structure of the forms was clearly defined and the pieces had tuneful melodies with accompanying harmonies following a well-organized progression from one key to another.

Classical oratorio composed by Antonio Salieri

Big C or little c?

The musical period between 1750 and 1820 is known as Classical with a capital letter "C", while the music traditions through history are known as classical with a lower-case "c".

The 18th century is known as the Age of Enlightenment, as great political and social changes occurred across Europe, leading to revolutions, industrial progress, and empire-building. A larger **middle class** was created who were interested in music and other arts.

Alessandro SCARLATTI (1660–1725)

The Italian composer Scarlatti wrote **overtures** for his operas in three sections, or movements: a quick one, a slow one, and another quick one. These elements were later to be seen in symphonies.

Musicians and composers became paid members of nobles' (**patrons'**) households. Composers now wrote (or notated) all parts for specific instruments. Their patrons demanded lots of music so often there was only time for one rehearsal.

In later life, Scarlatti also experimented with including more instruments in his music.

This early Classical sonata was composed by Domenico Scarlatti. He wrote 555 keyboard sonatas, demanding great musical virtuosity (brilliance) from the performers.

Domenico SCARLATTI (1685–1757)

Son of Alessandro, Domenico established the idea of a sonata as a piece for an instrumental soloist. He also developed the use of musical **ornaments** – fast notes close together played as a flourish in a melody.

C. P. E. Bach was one of the sons of J. S. Bach and an older brother to J. C. Bach.

A famous keyboard player, C. P. E. Bach bridged the change from the Baroque to the Classical style. He developed an expressive musical style known as the "**Empfindsamer Stil**" – changing the moods and emotions within a musical piece.

Carl Philippe Emanuel BACH (1714–1788)

In the Classical era, musical forms were established that would be used until the 1920s. **Sonata form** (not to be confused with the sonata) was a structure for a movement (section) in three parts:
• The exposition, where the main themes were introduced.
• The development, where the themes were developed by changing keys to build up a dramatic tension.
• The recapitulation, where the tension was resolved and the original themes returned to.

Gluck took **opera** in a new direction, away from the stilted plots and the soloists showing off. Instead, his operas, such as *Orfeo and Eurydice* (1762), developed a simple and dramatic storyline with strong characterization, where the music expressed the words and drama.

Christoph von GLUCK (1714–1787)

Classical composers wrote instrumental music for patrons and the people...

Middle Classical

Franz Joseph Haydn (1732–1809)

Fondly known as "Papa" Haydn, this Austrian composer established the symphony and the four-part **string quartet**. He was an inspiration for many future Classical composers.

Johann Christian Bach (1735–1782)

J. C. Bach became the music master to the British royal family. He established the lighter style of Classical music and organized many well-attended **public concerts** in halls.

Luigi Boccherini (1743–1805)

Italian-born, Boccherini was an outstanding cello player. He settled at the Spanish royal court, where he is particularly noted for composing five-part **string quintets** to include his cello or the Spanish guitar.

Late Classical

Antonio Salieri (1750–1825)

Born in Italy, Salieri went to Austria for his music training and was very influential on **Viennese court** music. He is sometimes portrayed as being jealous of Mozart's talents.

Muzio Clementi (1752–1832)

One of the first piano virtuosos, Clementi composed some dramatic and challenging **piano sonatas** (replacing the harpsichord). Whilst touring in 1781, he had a piano competition against Mozart (see page 48).

Luigi Cherubini (1760–1842)

The Italian Cherubini settled in Paris, where he became a leading conductor, composer, and teacher. He wrote in all sorts of styles, from comic to dramatic, and helped to develop the **French opera**.

Johann Nepomuk Hummel (1778–1837)

This gifted pianist was taught by Mozart for a couple of years. Along with Beethoven (see page 50), Hummel wrote innovative compositions, which were more **expressive** than early Classical music, and inspired future composers.

Samuel Wesley (1766–1837)

Nicknamed by some people as "the English Mozart", Wesley was an eccentric but very talented young musician. He wrote mainly church music and was particularly admired for his amazing **improvisations** played on the organ.

Jan Ladislav Dussek (1760–1812)

A Czech composer and virtuoso pianist, Dussek was the first to position the piano bench sideways, so that the audience could view him playing. His music was more **adventurous** in style than Mozart's, and used a longer keyboard.

47

Musician's biography

Wolfgang Amadeus **Mozart**

1756: *Born in Salzburg, Austria. His parents, Leopold and Anna Maria, had seven children but only two survived. Leopold was a musician in the court of the city's Archbishop.*

1761: *By five years old, composed minuets.*

1762: *Began four-year grand musical tour of Europe with his talented sister. Aged six, he played to the Austrian Emperor and Empress and aged seven years, played to the British monarchy.*

1768: *By age 12 years, he had written two one-act operas.*

1774–1777: *Mainly worked in Salzburg, composing.*

1779: *Appointed court organist in Salzburg, but the archbishop was jealous of Mozart's popularity and, after a quarrel, threw him out in 1781.*

1782: *In Vienna, aged 26, married Constance Weber. They had six children but only two survived, Karl and Franz. Although short of money, Mozart was happy working as a freelance composer.*

1791: *Died of typhus and kidney disease in Vienna aged 35 years, leaving a Requiem Mass unfinished. He was buried in a pauper's (poor person's) grave.*

Musician's influences

Johann Christian Bach (1735–1782)
Mozart met Bach in London in 1764–1765 (see page 47).

Franz Joseph Haydn (1732–1809)
Haydn perfected the classical sonata form and wrote string quartets (see page 47).

Wolfgang Amadeus Mozart

"Music, even in situations of the greatest horror, should never be painful to the ear but should flatter and charm it, and thereby always remain music."

Wolfgang Amadeus Mozart performing with his father and sister.

Piano developments

The piano was first invented around 1709 and developed throughout the 18th century (see page 62). Mozart's piano concertos helped to increase its popularity. The piano allowed the player to control how loud (forte) or soft (piano) the notes would sound.

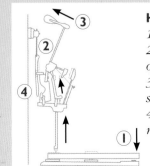

How a piano works
1. Key is pressed
2. Damper is lifted off the string
3. Hammer hits the string and rebounds
4. String vibrates to make the sound

From an early age, Mozart amazed everyone with his outstanding talent. He was recognized as a **child prodigy**, able to play the harpsichord by age four and composing music by age five. Mozart and Haydn were the masters of the mature **Classical** style. Mozart composed over 600 works in his relatively short life. His music not only showed his **brilliance** but also entertained a wide audience. Even today, many people consider him the greatest composer of all.

Mozart composing with Franz Joseph Haydn.

Le nozze di Figaro (The Marriage of Figaro) Act 2 finale

The Act 2 finale of *The Marriage of Figaro*, a part of which is shown here in Mozart's handwriting, builds up over nearly 20 minutes of **unbroken** flowing music. Mozart's music responds to the twists and turns of the **fast-moving comedy**, where the count is tricked by his wife, the chambermaid, and Figaro (a valet).

Mozart's operas

Opera was very popular during the Classical period, and Mozart composed more than 20 to earn some money. He used **clever narratives**, involving a main character such as a nobleman and a handful of other key characters, with a chorus and orchestra setting the mood of the scenes. He worked with a librettist, who wrote the words of the opera. His operas appealed to the public because they were **entertaining** and charming, blending comedy, melodrama, and sometimes **supernatural elements**. Mozart also conducted many of the performances.

Important operas

The Marriage of Figaro *(composed 1786) A comic opera about a devious count who tries to seduce his wife's chambermaid, but is found out.*

LISTEN TO TRACK 13
This is from the overture (beginning) of The Marriage of Figaro.

The Magic Flute *(composed 1791) The quest of a prince and a companion to rescue the ladies they love, helped by their magical instruments. This opera is a "singspiel", which includes both singing and spoken dialogue.*

Don Giovanni *(composed 1787) A dramatic opera about the downfall of a badly behaved nobleman, and his descent into hell.*

Harpsichord
The harpsichord was a very popular Baroque instrument. The strings were plucked when the keys were pressed, and the player could not control the volume.

Early piano
The strings are hit by hammers, which the player controls when striking the keys.

MUSICIAN PROFILE

Musician's biography
Ludwig van **Beethoven**

1770: *Born in Bonn, Germany. His father was a musician and forced him to practice the piano even into the night.*

1778: *Aged seven, gave his first recital.*

1787: *Aged 17, he travelled to Vienna to try to meet up with Mozart but was called back to Bonn where his mother was dying.*

1792: *Invited by Haydn, Beethoven moved to Vienna and established himself as a composer and the best piano virtuoso.*

1797: *Aged 27, he began to experience problems with his hearing. His hearing gradually deteriorated until he was completely deaf.*

1801: *Aged 31, Beethoven composed the* Moonlight Sonata.

1824: *The first performance of Beethoven's 9th symphony*

1827: *Aged 57, Beethoven died. 20,000 people lined the streets of Vienna to watch the funeral procession.*

Musician's influences

Wolfgang Amadeus Mozart (1756–1791)
The Classical style of Mozart was a powerful influence on Beethoven.

Franz Joseph Haydn (1732–1809)
Haydn was Beethoven's teacher and patron when he first went to Vienna.

LISTEN TO TRACK 14

Composed in 1795, Beethoven dedicated this Piano Sonata No.1 to Franz Joseph Haydn. The extract is from the 1st Movement, an Allegro, which means brisk and lively.

Ludwig van Beethoven

"Music should strike fire from the heart of man, and bring tears from the eyes of woman."

Beethoven composing at home in Vienna, Austria.

Symphonies:
A symphony is a long piece played by an orchestra. In his nine symphonies, Beethoven transformed the four-movement structure of the Classical symphony, extending its length and adding dramatic tension.

Beethoven's nine symphonies

	1st and 2nd Symphonies
PREMIERE DATE:	1800 and 1803
HEARING LOSS:	Partial deafness with buzzing sounds
DESCRIPTION:	Heavily influenced by the music of Mozart, Beethoven finds his musical feet.

Music from Symphony No.7 2nd Movement

Beethoven spent his life totally immersed in the world of music and is famous for breaking new ground in classical music. From a young age, he was hailed as a **child prodigy** in his homeland, Germany. Later, as an adult, he was the most sought-after pianist and composer in Vienna, the European capital of music. But what makes the man and his music exceptional is how through becoming deaf, which made him depressed, angry, and isolated, he expressed his feelings creatively through his music, influencing many later **Romantic** composers.

Napoleon Bonaparte (1769–1821)

Beethoven's hearing instruments

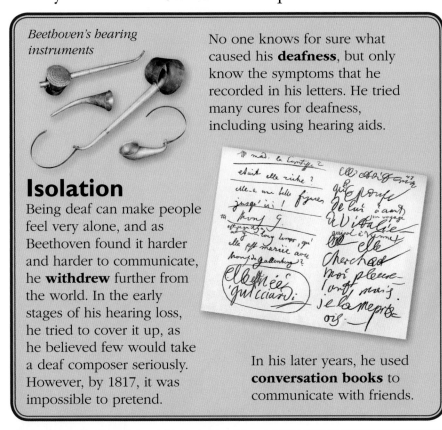

No one knows for sure what caused his **deafness**, but only know the symptoms that he recorded in his letters. He tried many cures for deafness, including using hearing aids.

Isolation

Being deaf can make people feel very alone, and as Beethoven found it harder and harder to communicate, he **withdrew** further from the world. In the early stages of his hearing loss, he tried to cover it up, as he believed few would take a deaf composer seriously. However, by 1817, it was impossible to pretend.

In his later years, he used **conversation books** to communicate with friends.

Revolutionary music

Throughout the decade in which Beethoven wrote his first eight symphonies, war raged in Europe. The French commander **Napoleon** and his armies fought almost every European power. At first, Beethoven admired Napoleon's **revolutionary** spirit and dedicated his third symphony to him but later, in anger, tore up this dedication on the title page when Napoleon crowned himself Emperor of France in 1804. In 1809, Napoleon seized Beethoven's hometown of **Vienna** in Austria. Beethoven lived under French occupation until 1813, continuing to compose. Napoleon was finally defeated in 1815 and exiled.

3rd Symphony	4th Symphony	5th and 6th Symphonies	7th and 8th Symphonies	9th Symphony
1805	1807	1808	1813 and 1814	1824
60% of hearing lost	Becomes more…	… and more deaf	Almost completely deaf and started to use hearing aid	Completely deaf
Dedicated to Napoleon (but later undedicated), this *Eroica* symphony revolutionized music itself.	Perhaps the least played of the nine symphonies, but masterful nonetheless.	The 5th is one of the most famous symphonies. The 6th is known as *Pastoral*. It's about the Austrian countryside.	The intense, funereal 7th reflects the Napoleonic wars that had ravaged Europe. The 8th is very bold and beautiful.	One of the greatest symphonies ever composed, combining orchestra with a chorus of singers.

Map of the orchestra

An orchestra is a large group of musicians playing together on various instruments. There could be 70 to 100 instrumentalists, depending on the music to be played. The orchestra developed gradually from the court bands of the 17th century. Instruments improved and new ones were added and, by about 1830, a typical **symphony orchestra** was complete.

A grand piano can be used as an orchestral or solo instrument (for piano concertos when it is usually positioned at the front of the stage).

Percussion

Tubular bells

Gong

Snare drum

Bass drum

Tambourine

Cymbals

Triangle

Brass

French horns

Woodwind

Bass clarinet

Piccolo

Clarinets

Flutes

Strings

Harp

Second violins

First violins

String section
String instruments have tightly stretched strings that vibrate to produce sound. There are four instruments varying in size from the smallest, the violin, to the largest, the double bass.

Percussion section

Many percussion instruments produce a sound when the musicians hit them, others are shaken. There are some that can be tuned to different notes, while others are untuned and have no fixed pitches.

Xylophone

Timpani (see page 91)

Trombones

Bass trombone

Seating arrangements

The players are seated in a semicircle facing the conductor. The louder instruments are positioned behind the quieter ones to produce a good balance of sound.

Brass section

Brass instruments are long metal tubes, coiled into different shapes. The trumpet makes the highest notes, the horns and trombones sound the middle notes, and the tuba makes the lowest notes.

Tuba

Trumpets

LISTEN TO TRACK 15

Listen to the ticking rhythm of this 2nd movement from Haydn's Symphony No.101, known as "The Clock". Make a list of the different instruments you can hear.

Bassoons

Contra bassoon

Woodwind section

Wind instruments produce sound by vibrating air down a tube. Set out in two rows, these instruments make a wide range of sound from the high-pitched piccolo to the low notes of the contra bassoon.

Oboes

Cor anglais

Violas

Double basses

Cellos

Conductor

Romantic (1815–1910)

The story continues…

The emotional and dramatic compositions of late Classical composers, such as Beethoven (see page 50), inspired a generation of Romantic composers. Music to the Romantics became a way of expressing their emotions and ideas. Inspired by nature and their country's music and history, they experimented with new rich harmonies.

Ludwig van Beethoven (1770–1827)

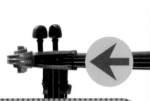

Louis SPOHR (1784–1859)
A German composer and violinist, Spohr influenced many Romantic composers by the way he combined the structured Classical forms with expressive and **rich-sounding harmonies**. He wrote more than 90 songs inspired by love poems. As a conductor, he was one of the first to use a baton.

Niccolò PAGANINI (1782–1840)
The Italian composer Paganini was an outstanding violinist. His technically challenging, imaginative, and well-crafted violin solos inspired later Romantic composers to use **instrumental brilliance** as a way of conveying expression in their music.

The beginning of the 19th century was the start of an age of exploration, discovery, and new scientific ideas, leading to the Industrial Revolution and empire building.

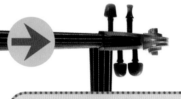

Signed score by Paganini, 1829

Franz SCHUBERT (1797–1828)
By age 17, Schubert was composing exciting and **adventurous melodies**, breaking away from the Classical style of the times and composing emotional and imaginative music more typical of the Romantic style. Although he died at only 31 years of age, he composed a huge amount of music, and is especially known for his **German art-songs** or Lieder – poems set to music for singer and pianist.

By the 19th century, the piano had developed its full, rich tone and became a popular instrument in the home. Brass instruments now had valves so they could play a larger range of music. Improved instruments gave Romantic composers a **greater variety** of sound.

Carl Maria von WEBER (1786–1826)
Weber's opera *Der Freischütz*, first performed in 1821, marked the beginning of German Romantic opera. Weber showed how opera could be based on **national** folk tales and folk tunes.

Romantic artists were also inspired by their country's landscapes. This painting, Mountain Out of the Mist, 1865, is by Albert Bierstadt.

Romantic composers were inspired by drama and poetry...

Early Romantic

Felix Mendelssohn (1809–1847)
Inspired by his musical sister, Fanny (1805–1847), Mendelssohn at age 17 wrote *A Midsummer's Night's Dream*, the first of his many concert **overtures**, or short orchestral works.

Frédéric Chopin (1810–1849)
A brilliant pianist, Chopin composed short, melodic pieces, including those based on **Polish dances**. He is famous for composing the *Minute Waltz*, which some pianists try to play in one minute.

Robert Schumann (1810–1856)
Like many Romantic composers, Schumann was influenced by literature, often referring to stories and poems as his themes for his piano works and **song cycles** (group of songs). His wife, Clara, was a great pianist.

Anton Bruckner (1824–1896)
This Austrian composer wrote nine famous large-scale symphonies. The **long sections** allowed his music to develop very slowly, giving the pieces a spiritual quality of sound.

César Auguste Franck (1822–1890)
A Belgian composer, Franck influenced the revival of the traditional structured symphony and the use of "**cyclic form**" in music, where several movements had themes linked to a main melody motif.

Franz Liszt (1811–1886)
Liszt, composer of *Hungarian Rhapsodies*, introduced the term "**symphonic poem**" for a large-scale, one-movement piece of music taken from a dramatic play, historical event, or mythology.

Middle and Late Romantic

Johannes Brahms (1833–1897)
A great German composer, Brahms rejected the new Romantic forms and composed masterpieces in the **Baroque and Classical style** developed from J. S. Bach to Beethoven.

Georges Bizet (1838–1875)
The short-lived French opera composer, Bizet is best known for his opera *Carmen* performed in 1875, which shocked audiences with its **lifelike characters** and realistic on-stage murder.

Richard Strauss (1864–1949)
Strauss was a masterful **storyteller**. He began his musical career by composing songs and symphonic poems, such as *Don Juan*, and ended composing great operas, such as *Der Rosenkavalier* (The Knight of the Rose).

Musician's biography

Hector **Berlioz**

1803: *Born at La Côte-Saint-André in France. His father was a country doctor and taught Berlioz.*

1815: *Aged 12, began studying music, teaching himself harmony, writing short pieces, and learning the guitar, flageolet, and flute. He enjoyed reading the works of Virgil (ancient Roman poet) and Shakespeare (English playwright).*

1821: *Aged 18, sent to Paris to study medicine, which he hated, but visited the Paris Opéra and the Paris Conservatory library and began composing.*

1824: *He abandoned medicine and two years later attended the Paris Conservatory to study composition.*

1831: *After winning the scholarship Prix de Rome and composing* Symphonie Fantastique, *he went to Italy to study for two years, before returning to Paris and producing more works.*

1842–1863: *Travelled throughout Europe and Russia conducting operas and orchestral music.*

1865: *Aged 62, published his memoirs.*

1869: *Aged 66, he died in Paris and was buried in Montmartre Cemetery next to his two wives.*

Musician's influences

Christoph von Gluck (1714–1787)
Berlioz admired Gluck's opera music, which he heard in Paris (see page 46).

Ludwig van Beethoven (1770–1827)
Berlioz was overwhelmed by the emotion of Beethoven's third and fifth symphonies (see page 50).

Hector **Berlioz**

"To render my works properly requires a combination of extreme precision and irresistible verve, a regulated vehemence, a dreamy tenderness, and an almost morbid melancholy."

Original and ahead of his time, Berlioz inspired many later Romantic composers. He **revolutionized** the sound of the orchestra with his instrumentation and began the Romantic idea of telling a story through music, known as programme music. He was not only a composer, but also a great conductor, writer, and critic.

Actress Harriet Smithson

Programme music

Berlioz transformed the symphony from a Classical structured form to a Romantic dramatic and emotional one. In 1830, he composed his famous and ground-breaking *Symphonie Fantastique.* The symphony told a story about the tortured dream of a despairing artist. Berlioz wrote his own **programme notes** explaining the scene for each of the five movements. He wrote the piece after seeing William Shakespeare's play *Hamlet* in 1827 and falling in love with the actress, Harriet Smithson, who played Ophelia. At first, she refused to meet him but, six years later, they married.

Orchestral effects

In the *Symphonie Fantastique,* Berlioz not only introduced a wider range of instruments into the orchestration but also used the instruments in an effective way to convey the dream-like and intense drama of the story.

Movement 1:
Daydream – Passion
The artist dreams of the girl he loves.

Violins and solo **flute** play the *idée fixe* – a theme returned to often throughout the whole piece. The theme rises and falls, representing the artist's feelings for the girl he loves.

Movement 2:
A Ball
The artist attends a party.

Two **harps,** playing the flowing waltz, represent the glamour and splendour of the ball.

Cornet solo expresses the guests having a good time.

Cartoon of Hector Berlioz questioning his experimental orchestration, 1846.

Orchestration

As Berlioz was self-taught in music and had studied works of other composers on his own, he intuitively knew how instruments could be combined. He wrote about the **range** and **quality** of the instruments and the role each one played within the orchestra in his *Treatise on Instrumentation*, published in 1844. In 1904, Richard Strauss revised the book to include more modern instruments.

Movement 3:
Scene in the Country
The artist wanders alone in the countryside.

A **cor anglais** and an **oboe** played offstage convey two shepherds talking in the distance.

Four **timpani** parts replicate a thunderstorm.

Movement 4:
March to the Scaffold
The artist poisons himself and dreams he is being executed for murdering his love.

Timpani and blazing **horns** are part of the march music to the scaffold.

Solo **clarinet** plays the last thoughts of the artist interrupted by a strong chord from the rest of the orchestra as the blade of the guillotine drops.

Movement 5: Dream of a Witches' Sabbath
The artist dreams of his funeral amid a gathering of dancing witches and monsters.

Violins played with the wood of the bows convey terror and an eerie effect.

Tubular bells are used to represent the tolling funeral bell.

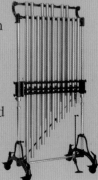

Outstanding operas

Dramatic and **extravagant**, operas have been transformed from the musical drama of *Euridice* by Jacopo Peri, first performed in 1600, to the epic and fantastic compositions of the Romantic composers. Today, operas are modern and **experimental**. Operas are expensive to put on as they involve lots of singers, instrumentalists, and scenery.

Opera styles Opera performance has developed in various ways. Two of the main styles are:
Grand opera – A large-scale opera on a serious theme with no spoken dialogue.
Opera buffa – Comic opera with silly plots and light-hearted music.

◄ Il Guarany, 1870, **Antonio Carlos Gomes**
This opera is named after a South American tribe, the Guarani. *Il Guarany* is a fast paced love story, set against a backdrop of tribal war.

► The Barber of Seville, 1816, **Gioachino Rossini**
This comic opera is a complicated love story where the barber, Figaro, helps his old master, Count Almaviva, win the beautiful Rosina.

LISTEN TO TRACK 16
This is the famous drinking song from the first act of the opera La Traviata.

▲ La Traviata, 1853, **Giuseppe Verdi** A tragic tale of the courtesan Violetta and her lover Alfredo. Alfredo's father disapproves of the relationship and forces the couple to part. When they are finally reunited, Violetta, who is incurably ill, falls dead at Alfredo's feet.

▲ Jenufa, 1902, **Leoš Janáček** This is the story of Jenufa, pregnant by Steva but loved by his jealous brother Laca. When the unmarried Jenufa has her baby, her stepmother is so ashamed she drowns it. Nevertheless, Jenufa and Laca put this tragedy behind them and start a new life.

▲ **Porgy and Bess,** 1935, George Gershwin
Porgy, a disabled beggar from the slums of South Carolina, USA, falls in love with a prostitute called Bess. This is their story.

▲ **The Vanishing Bridegroom,** 1990, **Judith Weir** There are three parts to this mysterious story. It begins with a missing inheritance.

▲ **Madam Butterfly,** 1904, Giacomo Puccini
Although Lieutenant Pinkerton marries a Japanese geisha girl, Butterfly, he does not intend to stay with her. When he leaves, she waits. He finally returns with his new wife and in grief, Butterfly kills herself.

◄ **Beijing opera,** late 18th century, China This type of opera incorporates music, singing, dancing, dialogue, and acrobatics.

◄ **Montezuma,** 1963, **Roger Sessions** This opera tells of Montezuma, the last great Aztec leader in Mexico, and his defeat by Spanish conquerors in the 16th century.

59

Musician's biography
Richard **Wagner**

1813: *Born in Leipzig, Germany, Wagner was the youngest of nine children. He largely taught himself music.*

1836: *Aged 23, married Minna Planer, which was to be a long stormy relationship ending in 1862.*

1839: *Aged 26, moved to Paris to avoid creditors. Wagner was poor so he worked as a music journalist.*

1842: *Successful first performance of his opera* Reinzi *in Dresden followed by* The Flying Dutchman *premiere in 1843. He became the conductor at the royal court in Dresden.*

1849: *Aged 36, after joining the rebelling Republicans, was forced to leave Germany for a long exile in Switzerland.*

1859: *Completed the epic musical love story of* Tristan and Isolde *but it was believed to be unplayable and not performed until 1865.*

1862: *Aged 49, he was allowed to return to Germany where the "mad" King of Bavaria paid off his debts and gave him a comfortable villa near Munich. There he finished his great work,* The Ring Cycle.

1883: *Aged 70, Wagner died of heart trouble and was buried next to his faithful dog, Russ, in the garden of his house in Bayreuth.*

Musician's influences

Ludwig van Beethoven (1770–1827)
Wagner said that it was Beethoven's music that turned him from being a writer to a musician.

Franz Liszt (1811–1886)
Liszt was Wagner's friend and mentor. Liszt helped him while in exile and promoted Wagner's music. Wagner even married Liszt's daughter.

Richard Wagner

"I write music with an exclamation mark!"

Wagner reinvented opera as **music drama,** combining poetry, drama, music, and art. He was also the first composer to create **every aspect** of his music dramas. He composed the music, created the plot and characters, and wrote all the words. (Other great composers had always left the lyrics to others.) He began his career writing plays and poetry, only turning to music after an illness. People either love his music or hate it, but no one denies his greatness.

Lohengrin, *1850, Opera in three acts*

Bayreuth Festival Theatre, opened 1876 for the first complete performance of *The Ring Cycle* over four nights.

Writer, composer, director...

Wagner was **revolutionary** as a composer because he created a complete work. He wrote everything, and gave the same importance to each part, from the staging to the music to the lyrics. He even went one step further by creating the **venue** for his opera. He built a theatre in Bayreuth, Germany, especially for performances of *The Ring Cycle*. It is still one of the best places to hear Wagner's operas.

Neuschwanstein Castle
Wagner's fairy-tale opera *Lohengrin* was so loved by King Ludwig II of Bavaria that he was inspired to build a **fairy-tale** castle, which he called Neuschwanstein (New Swan Stone) after the Swan Knight in the opera.

Wagner's no.1 fan
Wagner was Adolf Hitler's favourite musician – Hitler called him **"The Master"**. Hitler, head of the Nazi Party and Germany's political leader between 1933 and 1945, saw in Wagner's operas his own vision of Germany. He used to make his officers listen to endless Wagner recitals. This hijacking of Wagner's work by Hitler has added to the controversy about his music.

Wagner's great work
It took Wagner 22 years altogether to create the 18 hours of music that make up *The Ring of the Nibelung*. It is a cycle of four complete musical dramas known as *The Rhinegold*, *The Valkyrie*, *Siegfried*, and *The Twilight of the Gods*. A **nibelung** means dwarf. The ring was created by the dwarf Alberich, who stole the gold to make it from the Rhinemaidens in the river Rhine. The ring is magic, giving the owner the power to rule the world, and many **mythical characters** try to get hold of it. Finally, it is returned to the Rhinemaidens.

A musical epic
The Ring is an immensely detailed network of themes, called **leitmotifs**, each of which has some meaning: symbolizing a character, a concept, or an object. The themes in the music change as the ideas within the opera develop. *The Ring* is not merely a story about gods, humans, and dwarfs but is also about Wagner's thoughts on good and evil.

Handwritten score from *The Ring*, c.1880

LISTEN TO TRACK 17
This music is the beginning of Act 3 of the second opera of The Ring Cycle, The Valkyrie, *and is popularly known as "The Ride of the Valkyries". Listen for the leitmotif of "the ride", which is first played by the brass instruments in the orchestra.*

61

Grand pianos in history

c. 200: *According to tradition, the santur, a stringed instrument played with hammers from Persia (modern-day Iran), probably led to the invention of the hammered dulcimer, which in turn led to the creation of the clavichord and harpsichord.*

1300s: *First written records of the harpsichord – a stringed instrument that was plucked.*

1500–1700: *The clavichord and harpsichord were popular instruments in Europe.*

c. 1700: *The rich Italian Medici family owned a piano, probably made by Bartolomeo Cristofori.*

late 1700s: *Johann Andreas Stein invented an improved version of the piano called the "Viennese piano".*

1777: *John Broadwood, Robert Stodart, and Americus Backers designed a piano in a harpsichord case – the original "grand piano".*

early 1800: *"Double escapement" (repetition) action was invented in France by Sébastien Érard, allowing for keys to be played extremely fast.*

1843: *Patent for the first full iron frame for a grand piano.*

1853: *Steinway and Sons set up a prestigious piano company.*

Grand piano range

Over seven octaves

Grand piano

" [The piano is] able to communicate the subtlest universal truths by means of wood, metal, and vibrating air." Kenneth Miller – scientist

Known as the **"king of instruments"**, the piano has the widest range of notes of any instrument, covering over seven octaves. The word "piano" is short for **pianoforte**, meaning that the instrument can be played louder and softer in response to the player's touch on the keyboard.

The first grand pianos were played in the royal courts and **wealthy** households of Europe and many were painted with elaborate designs.

Who's the baby?

Grand pianos come in several sizes starting with the **baby grand**, which are 162 cm (5ft 4 in) or smaller in length, and ending with the **concert grand**, which can be up to 3 m (9 ft 10 in) long. The longer the piano is, the longer the strings are, especially the bass strings, giving the concert grand piano a rich tone and resonance.

STEINWAY & SONS

*The **soft pedal** makes the notes sound softer.*

*The **sostenuto pedal** allows the notes already played to continue, but the following notes sound normal.*

*The **loud** or **sustain pedal** makes the notes continue to sound.*

The action
When a key is pressed on the keyboard, it moves a felt-covered hammer that strikes a steel string, making it vibrate (see page 48).

The **soundboard** *lies beneath the strings and vibrates when the strings are played.*

The strings are held under tension by the **iron frame**.

The **strings** *are made of steel wire. The higher pitched notes have two or three strings, while the lower strings are wrapped in copper wire to make them heavier.*

The **black keys** – *the sharps (♯) or flats (♭) – were traditionally made of ebony wood.*

The **white keys** *were traditionally made of ivory.*

The **keyboard** *is the visible part of the action and the keys are now made of plastic.*

The pattern of white and black keys is repeated every octave.

C D E F G A B C D E F G A B

Octave

🎧 **LISTEN TO TRACK 18**
This is the opening of the piano with orchestra arrangement by Liszt of his Hungarian Fantasy – a selection of folk melodies.

Top pianists

Many Classical and Romantic piano works were composed by brilliant pianists, such as **Wolfgang Amadeus Mozart, Ludwig van Beethoven, Franz Lizst, Frédéric Chopin,** and **Clara Schumann**. Pianos have changed quite a lot over the last 300 years and the music of these composers sounded quite different from the way it sounds on a modern piano. **Vladimer Askenazy** from Russia, **Nelson Freire** from Brazil, and **Idil Biret** from Turkey are just a few of the many international 20th century pianists who were child prodigies.

In the USA, grand pianos have three pedals but in Europe they have only two pedals – the soft and the sustain.

One of the greatest jazz pianists, **Oscar Peterson** (1925–2007), was called the "Maharaja of the keyboard" by Duke Ellington (see page 94).

Dazzling dances

Music has **inspired dancing** since people could beat out a rhythm with a couple of sticks. Now music is written specifically for **different dance styles,** and is made with anything from a single instrument, or voice, to a full orchestra. The dances themselves have different costumes, steps, and techniques from the romantic waltz to the energetic Irish dance.

▲ **Coppélia**, 1870, **Léo Delibes** French composer Léo Delibes moved away from the fashionable romantic ballet of his time with *Coppélia*. This humorous tale of a mechanical doll includes energetic national dances and character dance.

▶ **Viennese waltz,**

18th century This ballroom dance is performed by two people who turn and turn around each other. Although different music can be used for the Viennese waltz, the best known piece is probably *On the Beautiful Blue Danube* (1866), one of many waltzes written by Johann Strauss the younger.

▲ **Love, the Magician**
El amor brujo, 1915,
Manuel de Falla This music was written for flamenco dance, then updated for symphony orchestra and ballet. It tells of a Spanish gypsy girl haunted by the ghost of her dead husband. When she dances a whirling fire dance with the ghost, he disappears into the flames.

▲ **Kabuki,** **17th century**
A form of theatrical Japanese dance-drama where all parts, including those of women, are played by men. The dancers wear elaborate clothes and bright make-up. The music has ever-changing rhythms and is made by instruments and voices.

▲ **Billy the Kid**, 1938, Aaron Copland
This ballet tells the story of outlaw Billy the Kid. It includes cowboy tunes and American folk songs.

▲ **Figure ice-skating**, 19th century
As well as being a form of dance, figure skating is also an Olympic sport. All types of music can be used for ice-skating. Single skaters or pairs perform jumps, spins, and lifts to the music.

▲ **Argentine tango,**
19th century In this passionate dance, performers hold each other close as they move to the music. Astor Piazzolla revolutionized the traditional tango in the 20th century, using jazz harmonies.

LISTEN TO TRACK 19
Listen for the strong, repetitive rhythm in this Latin American tango.

▲ **Irish dance**, c. 400 BCE
In this type of dance, dancers usually hold their upper body still and move their legs and feet rapidly. The music is lively and toe-tapping, often performed by a violin. In 1994, the Irish dance show *Riverdance* was a worldwide hit.

◄ **Brazilian carnival,** 17th century
The annual Carnival of Brazil happens just before Easter and, in big cities like Rio de Janeiro, people parade and party in the streets. They dress in extravagant outfits and dance the hip-shaking samba or soca to loud, rhythmic music.

65

Musician's biography

Pyotr Ilyich **Tchaikovsky**

1840: *Tchaikovsky was born into a wealthy family in Votkinsk in Russia. He was the second of six children.*

1854: *Aged 14, he took up composing in earnest after his mother died.*

1859: *Aged 19, he graduated from law school and became a clerk at the Ministry of Justice.*

1863: *Aged 23, he gave up his job to study at the St Petersburg Conservatory. He graduated from there after four years.*

1866: *Moved to Moscow to teach at the new Conservatory.*

1876: *Madame von Meck, a wealthy widow, became his patron. For the next 14 years, she gave him a yearly allowance of £600, permitting him to compose full time, but they never met.*

1877: *Aged 37, he composed* Swan Lake. *He suffered a nervous breakdown and went to Switzerland, then Italy to recover.*

1885: *Aged 45, lived in virtual isolation in the Russian countryside between European concert tours.*

1893: *Aged 53, Tchaikovsky died in St Petersburg, Russia, probably of cholera from drinking a glass of unboiled water.*

Musician's influences

Wolfgang Amadeus Mozart (1756–1791)
Tchaikovsky loved dance music and the minuets and country dances of Mozart were some of his favourites.

Robert Schumann (1810–1856)
Schumann's symphonies, choral work, and his Children's Album inspired Tchaikovsky.

Pyotr Ilyich
Tchaikovsky

"Truly there would be reason to go mad were it not for music."

One of the great Romantic composers, Tchaikovsky is the composer of the popular **ballets** *Swan Lake*, *The Sleeping Beauty*, and *The Nutcracker*, as well as many beautiful symphonies, concertos, and operas. He had a smattering of piano lessons as a young child, but it was when his mother died when he was 14 years old that, shocked and **heart-broken**, he turned to composing music.

Tchaikovsky's ballets

Tchaikovsky loved **danceable** music and raised the status of ballet music to previously unknown heights. However, this wasn't immediately obvious to everyone…

The Sleeping Beauty – a hit!

Much of the original production of *The Sleeping Beauty* exists today. So when you see it, the ballet dancers' performances are much the same as those made by the original performers in 1889. Tchaikovsky's brilliant music adds strong **emotion** to the ballet and has two main themes: the dark, heartless theme for Carabosse (the wicked fairy) and the sweet, gentle theme for the Lilac Fairy (who is in this scene below).

Swan Lake – demanding

When *Swan Lake* was first composed it was little performed, as conductors, dancers, and audiences thought it was too difficult to dance to. It remains one of the most **demanding** ballets to perform, but ballet dancers nowadays love to dance it – if they can dance that, they can dance anything!

The Nutcracker – a flop?

The Nutcracker is one of the most widely enjoyed and **best-loved** ballets in the world. Although it flopped at its first performance in 1892, it has continued to be performed, and is now a magical part of the Christmas season for children all over the world. Many more who have never seen the ballet know its music – the highlights are collected together as *The Nutcracker Suite*.

LISTEN TO TRACK 20

This is an extract from Swan Lake. *It is the music for the Pas de Deux, which is performed by the Swan Queen, Odette, and Prince Siegfried, who has fallen in love with her. Later in the ballet, the evil sorcerer, Von Rothbart, tries to stop them being together, and so they jump into the lake and become spirits.*

The Children's Album

Tchaikovsky dedicated these short piano tunes to his favourite nephew. The 24 easy pieces were intended to be played by children and have titles like *The Doll's Funeral, Mother,* and *Winter Morning.*

Music and the person

Tchaikovsky was naturally shy and retiring. He was prone to great self-criticism, and he sometimes tore up his music before anyone else had seen it. His **melancholic** personality led him to write music that is sad and emotional, but he also composed music that is among the most buoyant and brightest ever heard.

National music

Since the 19th century, some composers have used their music to celebrate the qualities and **identity** of their countries, such as the scenery and legends. They have expressed this by experimenting with the rhythms and melodies found in their country's **folk** songs and dances.

LISTEN TO TRACK 21

This is from Edvard Grieg's music for the play Peer Gynt. Choreograph a troll dance in the Hall of the Mountain King, getting quicker and quicker.

Illustration and lyrics from Oh, Susanna, *Stephen Foster*

American nationalism

America's folk music was revived through **Stephen Collins Foster's** folk songs about the lives of 19th century people. **Amy Beach** was inspired by the folk music of her European ancestors and **Louis Moreau Gottschalk** used the harmonies and rhythms of Afro Creole music. *The Stars and Stripes Forever* was one of many band marches by **John Philip Sousa**.

British nationalism

Traditional folk songs, the atmospheric British countryside, Tudor polyphonic music, and Victorian empire-building have inspired the orchestral works of British composers, such as **Edward Elgar, Gustav Holst, Frederick Delius, Ralph Vaughan Williams, John Ireland,** and **Arnold Bax**.

On the last night of the Proms (a series of concerts held each year in London since 1895), British music is celebrated including Edward Elgar's Pomp and Circumstance March No. 1 *sung to the words of* Land of Hope and Glory.

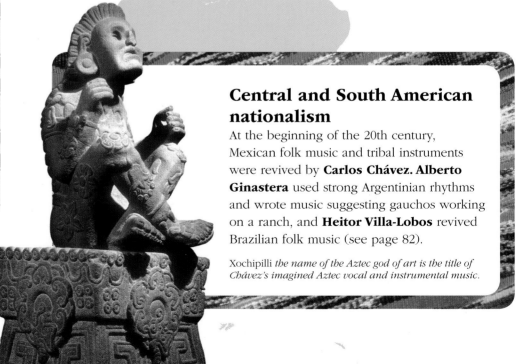

Central and South American nationalism

At the beginning of the 20th century, Mexican folk music and tribal instruments were revived by **Carlos Chávez. Alberto Ginastera** used strong Argentinian rhythms and wrote music suggesting gauchos working on a ranch, and **Heitor Villa-Lobos** revived Brazilian folk music (see page 82).

Xochipilli *the name of the Aztec god of art is the title of Chávez's imagined Aztec vocal and instrumental music.*

2006 performance of Peer Gynt Suite, *written 1875, Edvard Grieg*

Scandinavian nationalism

A distinctive Norwegian-style adventurous music was created by **Edvard Grieg** as heard in his *Peer Gynt Suite*. In Finland, **Jean Sibelius** used folk music and composed tone poems based on myths. The early 20th century Danish composer, **Carl Nielsen**, broke new ground with his six unique tonal symphonies that created tension.

A Life for the Tsar, *1836, Mikhail Glinka*

Russian nationalism

Except for folk music, most of the music in Russia at the beginning of the 19th century came from Europe. This changed when **Mikhail Glinka** developed Russian folk melodies in his opera *A Life for the Tsar*. Along with the "**Mighty Handful**" (see page 70), **Alexander Scriabin** and **Sergei Rachmaninov** used folk harmonies, themes from folklore with Russian characters, and sentimental, lively melodies.

French nationalism

French composers from the 19th and early 20th century, such as **Camille Saint-Saëns, Gabriel Fauré, Vincent d'Indy, Paul Dukas, Erik Satie, Maurice Ravel,** and **Francis Poulenc** have been influential in experimenting with harmonies, fantastical themes, and instrumentation. *The Swan* from the *Carnival of the Animals* by Saint-Saëns is one of the most famous classical pieces.

The Sorcerer's Apprentice, *1897, Paul Dukas, is based on a ballad about an enchanted broom.*

Smetana's Vltava *was a portrayal of the Vltava River in the Czech Republic.*

Spanish nationalism

Inspired by Spanish themes and people, national dances, such as flamenco (see page 27), and Spanish guitar harmonies, **Isaac Albéniz, Enrique Granados, Manuel de Falla,** and **Joaquín Rodrigo** (see page 98) were important composers in creating a Romantic Spanish style of music.

Dramatic paintings by Francisco de Goya, such as Bullfight in a Village, *c. 1812–14, inspired the piano suite and opera* Goyescas *by Enrique Granados.*

East European nationalism

Czech composers, such as **Bedrich Smetana, Antonín Dvořák** (see page 72) and **Leos Janácek** developed their country's musical style, creating pieces that portrayed the Czech landscape and used their language. Meanwhile, Hungarian composers **Béla Bartók** and **Zoltán Kodály** and Romanian **George Enescu** experimented with the themes and rhythms of their own country's folk music.

1855: *Aged 18, Mily Balakirev moved to Saint Petersburg, where he met, and was inspired by, the great composer Mikhail Glinka.*

1856: *Balakirev befriended César Cui and Modest Mussorgsky, who were both enrolled in the Russian army. He persuaded the two men to spend more time on their music.*

1857: *Glinka died. Balakirev took up the banner for Russian music.*

1858: *Mussorgsky gave up his army career to pursue his deepening interest in music.*

1861: *Balakirev met Nikolai Rimsky-Korsakov who combined a career in the navy with his music.*

1862: *Balakirev met chemist Alexander Borodin. Borodin and Rimsky-Korsakov started composing their first symphonies. Aged just 25, Balakirev founded Saint Petersburg's Free School of Music. He spent his summer travelling around the Caucasus and was greatly inspired by the folk music he observed there, returning to the region several times.*

1863: *Balakirev encouraged Borodin to give more time to music.*

Late 1860s: *The group started to squabble and drift apart, moving away from Balakirev's increasingly demanding influence.*

Musicians' influences

Mikhail Glinka (1804–1857)
The "Father of Russian Music", Mikhail Glinka encouraged a return to the real music of Russia.

Russian traditions
The "Mighty Handful" were often inspired by Russian legends, stories, songs, and folk dances.

The Mighty Handful

In the 19th century, a surge of nationalist feeling swept across Russia. Rather than continuing to mimic the styles of the West, Russian artists and composers wanted to create their own **sense of identity**. The "Mighty Handful" was a group of five composers who were all passionate about developing a distinctly **Russian music**.

The mighty five

The "Mighty Handful" came together with the aim of developing a uniquely Russian musical identity. The group worked on their music together, performing new compositions, engaging in long discussions, and suggesting alterations to each other's scores.

Mily Balakirev (1837–1910) was the group's leader. He was always encouraging the other composers, but he found it hard to finish writing his own compositions.

Modest Mussorgsky (1839–1881) lived a chaotic life and drank heavily. His music is much earthier than that of the other members of the group.

Alexander Borodin (1833–1887) was a chemist who wrote music on the weekends. He was the most romantic member of the group, famous for his lively choral music.

César Cui (1835–1918) composed operas and many songs for children. His music was inspired by Russian folktales and shows elements of Russian folk music.

Nikolai Rimsky-Korsakov (1844–1908) used lots of folk melodies and Russian themes, but he also understood and used Western styles of music.

A Russian folk group dances to Mussorgsky's *Night on the Bald Mountain*. This exciting music is about witches and demons gathering for the black Sabbath. It features wild cries and eerie, unsettling sounds.

🎧 **LISTEN TO TRACK 22**

This piece is known as the Flight of the Bumblebee from The Tale of Tsar Saltan. *The Swan-Bird has changed the Tsar's son into an insect so that he can fly to his father.*

The Tale of Tsar Saltan

Rimsky-Korsakov loved writing operas. His *Tale of Tsar Saltan* (shown above) is a magical story of romance and deception. It follows the fate of Prince Gvidon, who is marooned on an island after being thrown into the sea as a child. The opera features the *Flight of the Bumblebee*, Rimsky-Korsakov's most famous work.

Prince Igor
Borodin spent 18 years working on this opera, which was finished by Rimsky-Korsakov. It tells the story of a Russian prince who is captured by the Polovetsians and taken back to their desert camp. The opera features the famous Polovetsian dances, which are full of energetic leaps and whirls.

MUSICIAN PROFILE

Musician's biography
Antonín **Dvořák**

1841: *Dvořák was born the oldest son of the local butcher and innkeeper in a small village in Bohemia (in the present day Czech Republic).*

1857: *Aged 16, he entered music school in Prague, followed by the Prague National Opera orchestra (playing viola for conductors including Bedrich Smetana, Richard Wagner, and Franz Liszt).*

1874: *Aged 33, he won the Austrian State Music Prize for his compositions, judged by Johannes Brahms who became his great friend and mentor.*

1876: *Music publishers competed to buy Dvořák's work and international fame followed.*

1878: *First piano series of* Slavonic Dances *published.*

1892: *Aged 51, he became Director of the National Conservatory of Music in New York, USA.*

1895: *Dvořák suffered from homesickness in the USA and, after three years there, he returned to Bohemia.*

1901: *Dvořák's opera,* Rusalka, *was a critical success. He also became director of the Prague Conservatory.*

1904: *Dvořák died, aged 63.*

Musician's influences

Johannes Brahms (1833–1897)
Dvořák and Brahms were good friends and had a great admiration for each other's music.

Richard Wagner (1813–1883)
Dvořák was inspired when he played in a Wagner concert conducted by Wagner himself.

Antonín Dvořák

"I discover all that is needed for a great and noble school of music."

As well as music, Dvořák loved locomotive engines, ocean liners, and pigeon breeding.

Uplifting and upbeat, Dvořák was a breath of fresh air in the Romantic era. He was a master of the Germanic symphonic tradition, as well as a huge fan of the traditional folk music of his native **Bohemia** (now part of the Czech Republic). He successfully merged the two styles to create some beautiful music.

Bohemian roots

Antonín Dvořák's homeland, Bohemia, was under Austrian rule during his lifetime. Dvořák used the country's folk songs and dances, such as the **polka**, in his music to express the wish for **freedom** to have their own country.

Czech folk dancers

Carnegie Hall, New York, USA

Inspiring jazz

Dvořák wasn't in the USA for long, but he was quick to discover **African American music** and realized this was an important part of the American music tradition. He told the *New York Herald* in May 1893: In African American melodies, "I discover all that is needed for a great and noble school of music". A student of Dvořák's mentored a young Duke Ellington who became one of the greatest figures in **jazz history**.

From the New World

When Dvořák went to the USA to teach, his interest in **folk music** found an outlet in Native American music, and African American spirituals. Here, he composed his most famous work, *Symphony No.9 in E Minor* known as *From the New World*. This premiered to **rapturous** reviews at Carnegie Hall in 1893. The symphony is a beautiful combination of American-influenced sounds and Bohemian rhythms.

Astronaut Neil Armstrong took the *From the New World* symphony onto the Moon.

LISTEN TO TRACK 23

This is a solo trumpet arrangement of the main theme of the 2nd Movement of the From the New World *symphony.*

Duke Ellington (see page 94)

The Little Mermaid

One of Dvořák's greatest ambitions was to be a great operatic composer. He wrote **10 operas** but only *Rusalka* brought him the operatic glory he yearned and remains a firm favourite today. It partly follows the story of *The Little Mermaid* by Hans Christian Andersen.

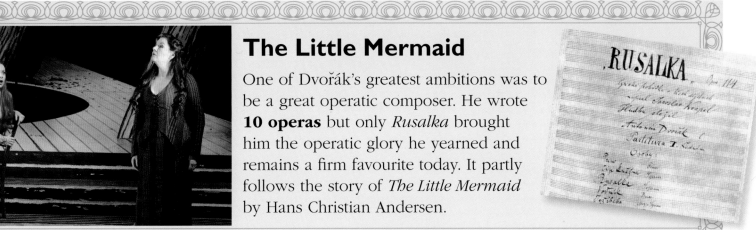

Great **conductors**

In an orchestra, a conductor's job is to make sure the musicians play when they should and keep in time. He also has to help the musicians convey the right feelings to an audience, such as joy or sorrow. The conductor leads the rehearsals and then directs the **performance**. Famous conductors each have their own style.

▲ **Hans von Bulow,** 1830–**1894, German** This pianist and conductor had a dominant manner that made some people fear him. He boosted the popularity of composers, including Richard Wagner.

▲ **Gustav Mahler,** 1860–1911, **Austrian** A leading conductor of his day, Mahler spent ten years at the Vienna Opera. He is also famous for the dramatic, emotional symphonies he composed.

▲ **Herbert von Karajan,** 1908–1989, **Austrian** Karajan became one of the most important musical figures of the 20th century. He spent 35 years as conductor at the Berlin Philharmonic Orchestra. During his career, he made over 800 recordings of almost all major classical works.

▲ **Pablo Casals,** **1876–1973, Spanish** Casals had a brilliant career as a cellist before taking up international-level conducting while in his 40s.

◀ **Georg Solti,** 1912–1997, **Hungarian-British** In 1995, Solti set up the World Orchestra for Peace. This included leading musicians from all over the world, who played together to show, in Solti's words, "the unique strength of music as an ambassador for peace."

LISTEN TO TRACK 24
Listen to this dramatic orchestral beginning, and then, in front of a mirror, imagine you are the conductor, using facial expressions and hand movements as you hear the piece again.

▲ **Simon Rattle,** 1955–, **British**
An award winning UK conductor, Rattle has conducted the City of Birmingham Symphony Orchestra and Berlin Philharmonic Orchestra. He is a popular recording artist.

▲ **Myung-Whun Chung,** 1953–,
Korean Born in Seoul, South Korea, Myung-Whun Chung is a pianist and conductor. He has worked with the world's leading orchestras, including the New York Philharmonic Orchestra.

A quick guide to conducting

A conductor holds the baton in front of him. He raises the baton and quickly swings it downwards – his signal to start.

His right hand twitches the baton up and down, keeping the beat of the music. This helps the players keep in time.

He uses his left hand to indicate how to play the music – smooth and flowing or strong and booming.

He uses facial expressions to strengthen the message of his left hand. This conductor wants the music to be played with short clear notes.

▲ **Marin Alsop,** 1956–, **American** Alsop is America's best-known female conductor. In 2007, she became the first woman to head a major US orchestra, when she took the job of Music Director at the Baltimore Symphony Orchestra.

▶ **Gustavo Dudamel,** 1981–,
Venezuelan Dudamel came from a poor family and learnt music through El Sistema, Venezuela's music education programme. A talented and charismatic artist, he has an energetic approach and brings out the detail in a musical piece. He is now Music Director of the Los Angeles Philharmonic Orchestra.

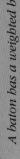

A baton has a weighted base...

... and wooden stick.

LISTEN TO TRACK 25

Imagine you are in a spaghetti western film riding into a ghost town as you listen to this piece for solo trumpet.

Triumphant trumpet

"Now the trumpet summons us again…"
John F. Kennedy – US President

People have been **blowing** into objects to make musical sounds since early times. The first trumpets were adapted from animal horns and seashells. The trumpet is the oldest of all the brass instruments, and is thought to be more than **3,500 years** old – although the early ones didn't have piston valves, which were added around 1815.

Trumpets in history

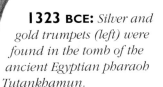

c. 1500 BCE: *Long, straight trumpets were used in China for signalling (carrying messages).*

1323 BCE: *Silver and gold trumpets (left) were found in the tomb of the ancient Egyptian pharaoh Tutankhamun.*

600 BCE–600 CE: *Roman armies (and many others since) announced their arrival on the battlefield with a terrifying trumpet blast. It roused the troops to battle, and frightened the enemy.*

1400s: *The first s-shaped trumpets were made, followed by "folded" and "slide" trumpets.*

1800s: *The trumpet was at its most popular. Mozart's father composed music for it.*

*Closing the **piston valves** makes the tube longer, producing different notes.*

To play the trumpet, players hold their lips taut and buzz them together as they blow into the mouthpiece. The air vibrates down the trumpet – which is really a bent tube of metal – and comes out of the bell.

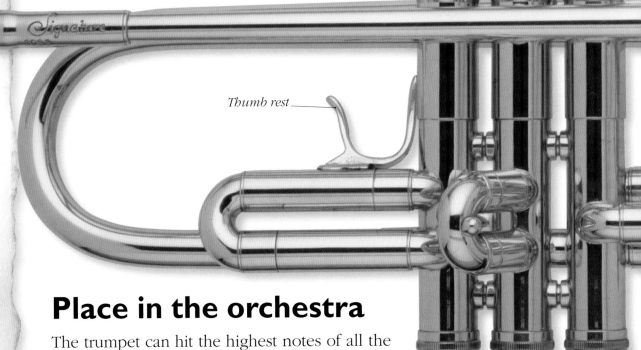

Mouthpiece

Thumb rest

Trumpet range

Over three octaves

Place in the orchestra

The trumpet can hit the highest notes of all the brass instruments. There are different types of trumpet; the most common is the B flat.

Trumpeter Hakan Hardenberger playing with the Swedish Chamber Orchestra at the classical music festival The Proms.

Top trumpeters

By the early 19th century, trumpets had become a fixed feature of the symphony orchestra. Famous modern classical trumpeters include Frenchman **Maurice André** and American **Adolph "Bud" Herseth**. Herseth played with the Chicago Symphony Orchestra from 1948 until 2001, and had an important influence on the modern orchestral trumpet sound. Today, the trumpet is also strongly associated with jazz through virtuosic players such as **Louis Armstrong, Chet Baker, Miles Davis, Wynton Marsalis, Arturo Sandoval, Guy Barker,** and **James Morrison**.

Jazz trumpeters are credited with developing different styles of trumpet playing. For example, "flutter tonguing", or rolling the tongue while blowing, makes a growling sound.

Bell

*The **fingerhook** helps the trumpeter hold the instrument steady and push down the valves at the same time with one hand, keeping the other hand free to turn pages and use mutes.*

Special effects

"**Mutes**" can be added to a trumpet's bell to change the sound. Jazz trumpeters often use the Harmon (or "wah-wah") mute, which produces a sound like a human voice. Hat mutes, which produce a softer noise, were originally bowler hats!

Papa Celestine uses his hat as a mute.

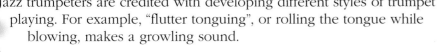

Cup mute   *Harmon mute*   *Straight mute*

Brassed off

Brass instruments are long hollow tubes that are blown into. Many have metal mouthpieces. In the 19th century, **valves** were added, allowing for a greater range of notes to be played.

How to blow?

Trumpet – Trumpeters buzz their lips as they blow into the mouthpiece, making the air inside vibrate.

By cutting off the pointed end of a triton shell, it can be turned into a horn, like the one here on Tanna island, South Pacific.

◀ Shells, c. 4000 BCE, worldwide Shells were used to make a simple form of early musical horns. Some are elaborately decorated with silver and semiprecious stones. Shell horns usually produce just one note.

▶ Shofar, c. 2000 BCE, Middle East One of the earliest Jewish musical instruments, the shofar is commonly used in religious ceremonies.

The shofar is made from the horn of a ram or other animal.

The Alpenhorn can be more than 4 m (13 ft) long.

▲ Alpenhorn, 16th century, Switzerland This long horn is usually carved from a solid piece of wood. It was originally used for communication between remote mountain villagers.

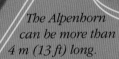

▼ Nafir, 1st century BCE, North Africa A long, loud blast from the nafir signals the end of the Muslim fast of Ramadan. As this 3 m (10 ft) brass trumpet is made in sections, it can be taken apart after use.

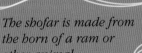

◀ Cor de chasse,
1600s, France This is
the French hunting horn.
It is made from a
coiled-up tube around
1.5 m (5 ft) long.

LISTEN TO TRACK 26
*This lively piece of music is
played by a brass ensemble.
Make your own trombone by
fitting together two long
cardboard tubes, one slightly
thinner than the other. Secure
with a rubber band, making sure
the smaller tube can slide up and
down as you buzz your lips over
the open end of the larger tube.*

◀ Sousaphone, 1898, USA
Named after the 19th century
American bandmaster, John
Philip Sousa, the
sousaphone (a type of
tuba) is a large
instrument commonly
used in marching
bands. The player
carries it on his
shoulders with the
bell held high. This
way the sousaphone's
loud, deep sound
travels up over the
heads of the other players
in the band.

▲ Trombone,
15th century, Europe
A player changes the
notes on a trombone by
moving the part called
the slide in or out. This
alters the length of the
tube, so changing the
pitch of the note.

Slide

▲ Serpent
**horn, 1590,
France** This deep-
sounding bass
instrument is called a serpent
horn because it looks like a
snake. It is a cross between
brass and woodwind, with a
brass mouthpiece and wooden
body with finger holes like a
woodwind instrument.

◀ Bazooka, c. 1910,
USA Invented by radio
comedian, Bob Burns, the
bazooka was made from old
pipes and funnels. It has a
slide-type device, like a
trombone, that alters the
pitch of the note as it is played.

*Comedian and talented brass player Bob Burns
holding a bazooka.*

Musician's biography
Claude **Debussy**

1862: *Born near Paris, France. His father was a shopkeeper and he was taught at home by his mother.*

1874: *Aged 10, he began music studies at Paris Conservatory.*

1884: *Aged 22, won the Grand Prix de Rome, a music scholarship, which allowed him to study in Rome for the next two years.*

1889: *First heard a gamelan (see page 28) playing at the Paris Exposition, and realized a single instrument could be just as effective as a full symphony orchestra, shaping the way he composed.*

1894: *At age 32, he wrote* Prélude à "L'après-midi d'un faune", *his first orchestral masterpiece.*

1902: *At age 40, premiere of his only completed opera* Pelléas and Mélisande, *which had five acts linked by orchestral interludes as if one long piece.*

1908: *Married for second time to Emma Bardac and composed* Children's Corner *for their daughter, Claude-Emma.*

1913: *Performance of last orchestral work, a ballet or dance-poem called* Jeux (Games), *which contained some of his strangest harmonies.*

1918: *Died aged 56 after a long battle with cancer.*

Musician's influences

Frédéric Chopin (1810–1849)
Chopin's passionate and complex piano melodies were typical of the late Romantic style.

French Impressionist artists
These artists, such as Claude Monet, aimed to paint an impression of their subject rather than the reality.

Claude **Debussy**

"It is unnecessary for music to make people think... It would be enough if it made them listen."

Claude Debussy with his daughter, Claude-Emma

Chou-Chou and the *Children's Corner* suite
Debussy affectionately nicknamed his daughter Chou-Chou and she was his inspiration for many of his works. In 1908, Debussy wrote a group of **six piano pieces** in a suite (set) called *Children's Corner*. The light, fun, but tricky-to-play, music about dancing, sleeping, and playing, captured the innocence and **wonder** of childhood.

In the **late 1800s**, the French composer Claude Debussy changed the direction of classical music with his very different approach. Known as an **"impressionist"**, Debussy used floating harmonies, shimmering passages of notes, and delicate tones in his compositions to create a **mood** or **atmosphere** when listening to his music. The overall effect of his music was of a **dreamy** impression.

Debussy entertaining his friends

A new harmony

Debussy's musical style was different from an early age. Debussy went to the Paris Conservatory to study music, however, he did not follow the classical rules and his teachers considered his atmospheric and **untraditional** approach to be dangerous. Although he was not a piano virtuoso, his playing was described as being **enchanting** and his many piano compositions, such as *Suite bergamasque*, required the player to use the pedals and keys skilfully to create flowing sounds and textures from the piano. He **experimented** with Asian-inspired scales and used chords just to set a mood rather than for dramatic effect, paving the way for further new directions in the 20th century.

Artwork by Leon Bakst inspired by Debussy's
Prélude à "L'après-midi d'un faune".

Preludes

In 1894, Debussy caused a stir in the music world with his *Prélude à "L'après-midi d'un faune" (The Afternoon of a Faun)*. Inspired by a poem, this prelude (a short introductory instrumental piece) features a loosely **flowing flute** melody that depicts the dreamy thoughts of the faun playing on his pan-pipes. He used no trumpets, trombones, or timpani, instead choosing instruments that kept the music **gentle**. The piece is known as a prelude as Debussy had intended to write two more pieces as part of a suite.

Drawing of faun costume for *"Le Faune"* ballet

LISTEN TO TRACK 27

This is a harp arrangement of the third movement from the Suite bergamasque *(1890) known as* Clair de lune *(moonlight).*

CLAIR DE LUNE

Poésie de
Paul VERLAINE

CHANT   Andantino

Musique de
Cl. DEBUSSY

PIANO

Musician's biography
*Heitor **Villa-Lobos***

1887: *Born in Rio de Janeiro, Brazil. His father, Raul Villa-Lobos, encouraged Heitor to play the cello, guitar, and clarinet.*

1899: *Raul Villa-Lobos died, leaving the 12-year-old Heitor to support his family. He earned money playing music in cafés and theatres around the city.*

1905: *Aged 18, Heitor journeyed into Brazil's interior, collecting folk music on his travels.*

1906–1907: *Played with Rio's street bands while studying for a short time at the National Institute of Music.*

1912: *Aged 25, took another trip into Brazil's interior to discover the music of the Amazon. Then married the pianist Lucilia Guimaräes.*

1923: *Won a government grant to study music in Paris. He used the trip to promote his exotic sound in Europe, where he was met with much interest and acclaim.*

1930: *Aged 43, returned to Brazil where he was appointed as director of music education in 1932 by the new nationalist government.*

1945: *Founded the Brazilian Academy of Music and was elected as its first President.*

1959: *He suffered from poor health in his later years and died at his Rio de Janeiro home aged 72.*

Musician's influences

The Ballet Russes
The dance company first visited Brazil in 1917, introducing Villa-Lobos to the music of Igor Stravinsky.

Arthur Rubinstein (1887–1982)
The talented pianist was a lifelong friend.

Heitor Villa-Lobos

"I learned music from a bird in the jungles of Brazil, not from academies."

The best-known and single most important Latin American composer, Heitor Villa-Lobos is famous for introducing **Brazilian folk music** and **Latin rhythms** to the world of classical music. A passionate character, quick to laugh and smile, he was very popular in his home country, where he reformed the music education system and promoted Brazil's rich musical heritage.

Villa-Lobos spent many years travelling around Brazil's interior studying the country's folk music. Later in his life, he told **wild stories** about his adventures, embellishing on the truth and inventing tales about his capture and escape from cannibals.

The uirapuru appears in many Brazilian myths and is seen as a symbol of good luck.

The mysterious Amazon rainforest

A gradual appreciation

The early work of Villa-Lobos was not well received by the people of Rio de Janeiro. In July, 1922, a performance of *Prole do Bebê* was met with boos. Villa-Lobos is reported as saying, "I am still too good for them." The piece was later declared to be "…the first enduring work of Brazilian **modernism**."

Heitor Villa-Lobos composed extensively, writing more than **1,500 pieces**, including concertos, symphonies, and chamber music, as well as music for string quartets, operas, ballets, and film scores. His works included using Baroque forms. Some of his critics say that he wrote too much and did not spend enough time "polishing" his work.

Uirapuru

Written in 1916, *Uirapuru* is an orchestral work that was inspired by Brazilian folk tales about the uirapuru, a small bird that lives in the **Amazon rainforest**. Famous for its complex, beautiful song, the uirapuru, or musician wren, features in many of the myths of the native Guarani people. Using instruments such as the quirky **violinophone**, Villa-Lobos composed a dramatic tone poem, in which the music mimics the mysterious sounds of the jungle.

A still from *Green Mansions*, a film starring Audrey Hepburn for which Villa-Lobos wrote a part of the score.

Heitor Villa-Lobos on a Brazilian banknote.

National pride

As the Brazilian government's director of music education, Villa-Lobos designed a **new system** of musical instruction for Brazilian children. He arranged lots of concerts and composed national and patriotic music for big choirs and public performances. His choir in 1935 had 30,000 voices and 1,000 instrumentalists. The impact of his work continues to make his country proud.

Hilarious operettas

Short light operas called **operettas** were the forerunner to musicals. Since the form originated in France in the mid-1800s, composers have produced memorable operettas with comic plots, fast action, light-hearted music, and spoken dialogue.

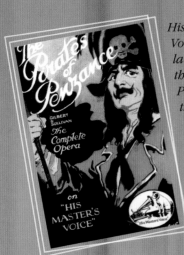

His Master's Voice record label recorded the Pirates of Penzance in the 1920s.

▶ Orpheus in the Underworld, 1858, Jacques Offenbach

Based on a Greek myth, this is the tale of Eurydice who is married to Orpheus but in love with a shepherd boy. The shepherd turns out to be a god who carries her off to the land of the dead. Orpheus then has to rescue her. The tune of the underworld gallop is more familiarly known as the "Can-Can".

2009 production of Orpheus in the Underworld *at Aix en Provence Festival, France*

▼ Pirates of Penzance, 1879, W. S. Gilbert and Arthur Sullivan

This story of tender-hearted pirates begins at a party for Frederic, celebrating his promotion to fully fledged pirate. However, Frederic wants to leave the pirates. He shouldn't be a pirate anyway – he should be a ship's pilot. His nurse misheard where to take him when he was a boy.

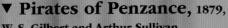

▲ Die Fledermaus, 1874, Johann Strauss the younger

This light-hearted story of revenge involves a party, a prison, and mistaken identity. The reason for revenge? A practical joke played on Dr Falke forced him to walk through the town in fancy dress costume. He was dressed as a bat – *die Fledermaus* in German.

▼ Véronique, 1898, André Messager Considered the

most successful of Messager's operettas, Véronique is about a heiress who becomes a flower shop girl to take revenge on a poor aristocrat Vicomte Florestan who does not want to marry her. By the end, they have fallen in love.

◄ Naughty Marietta,

1910, Victor Herbert A countess, Marietta, runs away from her home in France to New Orleans in the New World (USA). She hides her real identity, falls in love, is recognized by a villain who wants to marry her, but happily ends up with the man she wants.

◄ Frau Luna, 1899,

Paul Lincke Written by a German composer, Frau Luna (Mistress Luna), is about a trip to the Moon in a hot-air balloon. The music is lively and rousing.

The Merry Widow *performed in Sydney, Australia*

► The Merry Widow,

1905, Franz Lehar The widow in the title is Hanna Glawari, the wealthiest person in the country of Pontevedro. The problem is that Pontevedro will be ruined if she marries a foreigner and takes away her money. So the matchmaker, Baron Mirko Zeta, sets about finding her a local husband. Who will she choose?

Modern music

(1900–)

At the beginning of the 20th century, the self-taught Austrian composer Schoenberg was about to take Western classical music in a completely **new direction**. He didn't care about composing for popular taste, but instead was set on developing new techniques to **express emotions** and drama in his music. His life was a struggle and his works were mostly criticized during his lifetime, but they would later be an inspiration to future composers.

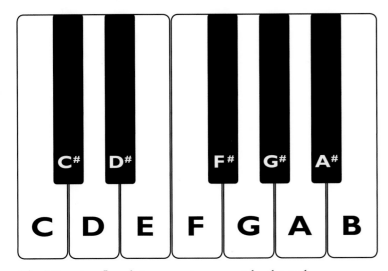

The 12 notes (keys) in an octave on a keyboard

Eerie music

Unlike previous Western music, the music of *Pierrot Lunaire* is not set in any key and has no tonic – usually the first note of a musical scale. This system is called **atonal** and makes the music feel unsettled and strange to the listener, which is ideal for conveying the image of a strange clown in the moonlight. Eight years later, Schoenberg was to invent a system of composing using **all 12 notes** in an octave, making all the notes of equal importance.

The use of **sprechstimme** is indicated on a score using small crosses through the notes' stems or the note-heads.

Expression through painting

From 1907, Schoenberg tried to express his emotions and ideas through painting, just as professional artists were doing at this time. He later gave up painting as he found that he could express himself better through his music.

Hatred, undated, by Arnold Schoenberg

Gershwin painting Schoenberg, 1936

Schoenberg was a keen tennis player and often played with his composer friend George Gershwin (see page 59). He also feared the number 13.

A large ensemble

Premiered in 1913, *Gurrelieder*, meaning Songs of Gurre, is a cantata for a huge orchestra, four choirs, five soloists, and a narrator. Based on poems by Danish novelist Jens Peter Jacobsen, the work is about a Danish medieval romantic and **tragic legend** set at Gurre Castle in Denmark. Schoenberg began writing this piece as a passionate young man but, by the time he had finished, not only had the piece grown, but also his composing style had also matured.

First page of Gurrelieder

Jens Peter Jacobsen (1847–1885)

Fun with drums

In the 20th century, musicians began experimenting with **percussion** instruments and using rhythm in new ways in both classical music and the emerging popular music. However, one of these groups of percussion, the drums, has been used around the world since prehistoric times and appears in all shapes and sizes. Known as **membranophones**, drums make a sound when the stretched membrane is struck with an object, such as a rounded stick or the tips of fingers.

How does a drum make a sound?

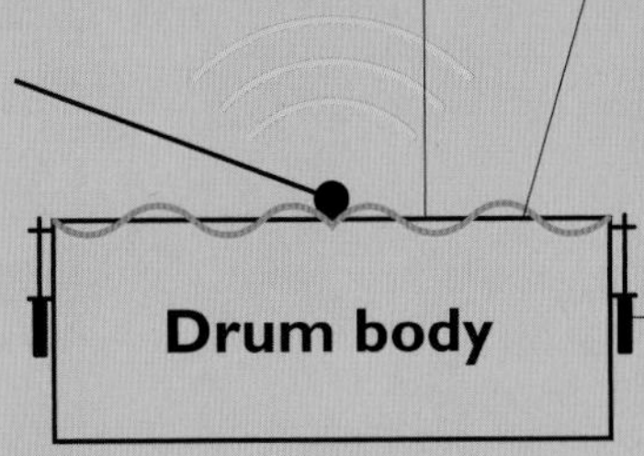

Membrane – The membrane is stretched over the drum body.

Vibration – When the membrane is struck the vibrations make the sound.

Drum body

Pegs – These can stretch or loosen the membrane, changing the sound.

◄ **Drum kit, 1930s, USA** To play this collections of drums and cymbals, drummers hold beaters or brushes in their hands, and operate pedals (bass drum and hi-hat cymbals) with their feet.

Hanging toms

Hi-hat cymbal

Floor tom

Snare drum

Brush   Mallet   Stick

Bass drum

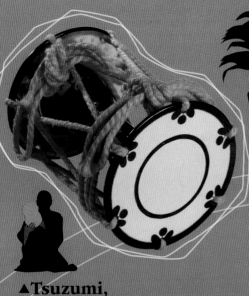

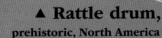

▲Tsuzumi,

c. 7th century, Japan This hourglass-shaped drum has cords attached to each end. Players tap it with their hands, squeezing or releasing the cords to alter the pitch.

▲ Rattle drum,

prehistoric, North America Rattle drums, with pellets inside, were used by native Americans during their ceremonies to honour the spirits of animals and trees.

▲ Tabor, 13th century, Europe

A two-headed drum that a player taps with drumsticks. This type of drum makes a crisp rat-a-tat-tat sound popular in military bands.

▶ Darbuka, ancient,

Middle East The goblet-shaped darbuka is a single-headed drum played with the hands. Its music is traditionally used by belly dancers.

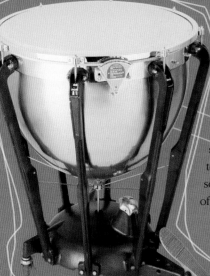

◀ Timpani, 13th century,

Middle East Sometimes called kettle drums, timpani are orchestral percussion instruments. Modern timpani have a foot pedal system to tighten or loosen the tension of the membrane, so altering the pitch of the note.

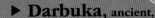

▼ Pellet drum,

date currently unknown, Asia Half drum, half rattle, this Asian instrument is used as a toy, or rattled by street vendors to attract attention.

▼ Bongos, 19th century, Cuba

These are two single-headed drums, one larger than the other, that are attached together. They are used in lively Latin American music such as salsa.

▲ West Indian steel drum, 1930s, Trinidad

Different areas on this metal drum make different notes. So, unlike other drums, it can be used to play a tune.

LISTEN TO TRACK 28

This is a piece of Caribbean music played on steel drums. The first steel drums were made from thrown away cans. Make your own using an empty can. Divide the can in three parts with a marker pen. Then, in one area at a time, use a small hammer to dent it slightly and test the sound by hitting the area with a wooden spoon. Make each area a different pitch.

The blues

 How did it happen?

Blues music grew from the folk music of black slaves in the southern states of the USA. Blues songs are very emotional, featuring **sad themes** with simple tunes typically based around three chords. During the 20th century, the blues became a strong influence upon the development of most popular music.

The Atlantic slave trade

By the 1700s, many millions of people from West and Central Africa were being taken from their homelands across the Atlantic Ocean to work as slaves on plantations in the West Indies and the USA.

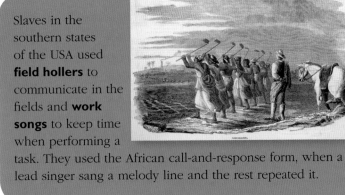

Slaves working on a sugar plantation in the West Indies.

Slaves in the southern states of the USA used **field hollers** to communicate in the fields and **work songs** to keep time when performing a task. They used the African call-and-response form, when a lead singer sang a melody line and the rest repeated it.

Slaves expressed their suffering and hope for a better life through the singing of **spiritual** songs. African rhythms and harmonies were combined with Christian songs. Through humming, clapping, and altering the pace, variations of the melody line were repeated over and over.

In 1862, the **Emancipation Proclamation** stated that from 1 January, 1863, all slaves in the southern states were free. The people spread north to cities across the USA, taking their music with them.

Cover of sheet music for Laughing Song

The **first African American recording** was in 1895, with George W. Johnson's *Laughing Song*. It was promoted as "race music". At the time, there was racial segregation and race music was recorded by black people for black people.

Freed slaves spread across the USA in 1863.

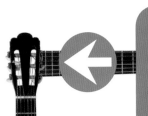

W. C. Handy (1873–1958)

In 1903, while waiting at a train station in Mississippi, the musician W. C. Handy overheard a man singing while scraping a knife across a guitar. The sound – known as a slide guitar – influenced Handy to write some of the first **folk blues** music.

Ma Rainey (1886–1939)

Ma Rainey was part of a travelling minstrel group, performing in cities across the USA. In the 1920s, she was one of a number of female blues singers to record their **classic blues** music.

As blues singers moved about, a range of regional styles developed and evolved from the use of acoustic to electric guitars as the lead instrument...

Country blues

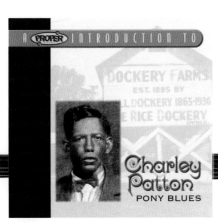

Delta blues

Charles Patton (1891–1934), known as the father of the Delta blues, came from the very poor area of the Mississippi delta. He often played loudly on an acoustic slide guitar in strange positions and sang in a rough voice about hard times.

Texas blues

In the 1920s, **Blind Lemon Jefferson** (1893–1929), known as the father of the Texas blues, played with a more relaxed, swing feel. He had a high-pitched voice and used guitar solos, known as "licks", within his songs.

Memphis blues

Performers in a **jug band** played with a range of homemade instruments such as a kazoo, a washtub for bass, a jug, and a whisky bottle, as well as a banjo, harmonica, or guitar.

New Orleans blues

New Orleans blues, as played by **Professor Longhair** (1918–1980), can be recognized for its upbeat cheerful Caribbean rhythms played on either a piano or a horn, rather than a guitar or a harmonica.

Louisiana blues

Louisiana blues, or Swamp blues, as played by **Lightnin' Slim** (1913–1974), has a laid-back, simple guitar style and slow rhythms, which makes the music feel dark and foreboding.

Piedmont blues

Piedmont blues, or East Coast blues, became a distinctive finger-picking method of playing the guitar. The style used by **Blind Boy Fuller** (1907–1941) also has highly syncopated, ragtime rhythms.

Electric blues

Chicago blues

In the 1950s, **McKinley Morganfield** (1915–1983), nicknamed Muddy Waters, amplified his guitar to play the Delta blues in a more striking way. Drums, bass, piano, and saxophone played with the guitar and harmonica in this blues.

Blues rock

Chester Arthur Burnett (1910–1976) was known as Howlin' Wolf due to his powerful booming voice and large imposing figure. The blues rock sound combined the three-chord blues with boogie rhythms and rock-and-roll style.

Soul blues

Developed in the 1960s, soul music is a combination of R&B (rhythm and blues), gospel music, and traditional blues style. The blind singer and pianist, **Ray Charles** (1930–2004), wore trademark dark glasses.

MUSICIAN PROFILE

Musician's biography
Duke **Ellington**

1899: *Edward Kennedy Ellington was born into a middle class African American neighbourhood in Washington D.C., USA.*

1906: *Aged seven, he began piano lessons.*

1914: *By age 14, he had composed his first two pieces* Soda Fountain Rag *and* What you Gonna Do When the Bed Breaks Down. *His friends nicknamed him Duke because he was always so stylish and polite.*

1917: *Aged 18, he formed his first group, The Duke's Serenaders, playing at dance halls for $5. By 1923, Duke had moved to New York, playing in various clubs with his band, now renamed The Washingtonians.*

1927: *Ellington and his band played at the Cotton Club in New York, and found an international audience.*

1930s: *Duke and his band left the Cotton Club in 1931 and toured the USA and Europe. They were now an established swing band, and the 1930s was their heyday.*

1940s–1950s: *The band reached a creative peak in the early 1940s. Ellington's Orchestra survived new developments in jazz and, in 1956, had gained new audiences.*

1960s: *He and his band played with top musicians like John Coltrane, Ella Fitzgerald, Louis Armstrong, and Frank Sinatra (see page 102).*

1974: *Aged 75, he died of cancer. 12,000 people attended his funeral.*

Musician's influences
Harvey Brooks (1899–1968)
A ragtime pianist whom Duke Ellington met as a young boy, and who showed him piano-playing techniques that were loose, free, and inspiring.

James "Bubber" Miley (1903–1932)
An early experimenter on the trumpet, his style changed the sound of Ellington's band to one that was hotter and more contemporary (and less "sweet").

Duke **Ellington**

"I try to catch the character and mood and feeling of my people."

Duke Ellington in New York, USA, in 1973

Sophisticated, polite, handsome, and elegant, Duke Ellington was one of the most **influential** figures in jazz – and American – music. Although he was a gifted pianist, this was the age of the **big band**, so he composed band music with huge success. He had one of the longest lasting careers of any **jazz** musician and, crucially, he was able to adapt to the times to be a musical influence throughout the ups and downs of the 20th century, from the age of swing to the 1960s social revolution.

Duke Ellington was so **stylish**, well-mannered, and handsome that he attracted the attention of film makers, and he and his band appeared in several films during the 1930s, such as *Black and Tan*.

Duke Ellington with his big band orchestra in 1942

A long playlist

If you wanted to play all of Duke Ellington's compositions, you'd be doing it for a long time! He composed over **1,500 songs**, scored the soundtrack on many films, and also wrote jazz "suites" that lasted over an hour. You would also need a big band and talented players. Duke Ellington hired and featured some of the greatest, most **creative players** of the time, including the alto saxophonist Johnny Hodges, the trombonist Joe "Tricky Sam" Nanton, and the trumpeter Cootie Williams. It would be worth it though, as then you could hear his hits, including *It Don't Mean A Thing If It Aint Got That Swing* and *Solitude*.

The Cotton Club

In 1927, Duke Ellington and his band became the house band at the Cotton Club – the most famous nightspot in **Harlem**, the black neighbourhood of New York. However, the Cotton Club would only let white people in. Eventually, the club did relax its white-only policy slightly, at a request from Ellington. His **broad appeal** meant he was able to break down racial barriers.

Live radio broadcasts went out from the Cotton Club to all of the USA.

LISTEN TO TRACK 29

This is the sound of a big band playing jive – a lively dance style, similar to swing music, that originated in the USA in the early 1940s.

Ellington had huge success.

Power of music

In the 1920s and 1930s, the USA was still a country of racial discrimination where black people were often segregated from white people. Ellington became one of the leading jazz artists in the 1930s to make open political statements, protesting about this situation in his music.

Inside the Cotton Club, 1937

Know your jazz

Duke Ellington lived through the **"Age of Jazz"**, when different types of jazz were in their early development. Combining African-influenced music with European melodies and instruments, the first generation of free black Americans (including people like **Scott Joplin** who composed *The Entertainer*) brought their music to the American public.

Boogie-woogie

A type of piano-based blues, boogie-woogie is blues that you can dance to!

Pianist Mary Lou Williams playing boogie-woogie music.

Syncopation

Fundamental to jazz, this is music where stressed beats (that aren't usually stressed) give a piece its all-important rhythm.

St. Paulite Arma Milch leads the female jazz band, the "Queens of Syncopation", in 1929.

The blues

An influence in the development of jazz, the blues portrays emotions, and is identifiable by its distinctive scale and set of chords (see page 92). Ray Charles

Ragtime

"Ragged" (syncopated) rhythm gives ragtime its name. It was the precursor to jazz, popular between 1897 and 1918.

Ragtime pianist Eubie Blake (1883–1983) with singer Noble Sissle (1889–1975)

Swing

A type of jazz you just can't help tapping your feet to, swing was played by big bands in the 1930s. It has a rhythmic "feel" or "groove" and people danced to it.

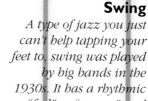

Sassy saxophone

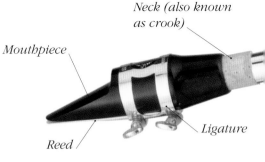

Neck (also known as crook)

Mouthpiece

Ligature

Reed

"Don't play the saxophone. Let it play you."
Charlie Parker

Originally invented over **150 years** ago in Paris for use in military bands and orchestras, this impressive woodwind instrument, usually made of brass and more popularly known as the "sax", was never really taken up by composers as an orchestral instrument. Instead it was embraced wholeheartedly by **jazz** and **swing bands**, becoming popular as a solo instrument, and nowadays plays a part in most styles of music.

Saxophones in history

Early 1840s: *A Belgian instrument maker, Adolphe Sax invented the saxophone in Paris. He combined a clarinet-style reed and mouthpiece with a key system from the oboe and flute, and the conical brass body of the "ophicleide", a popular brass instrument of the time. The saxophone could project sound like a horn, while having the versatility of a woodwind instrument.*

1844: *The composer Hector Berlioz (see page 56) featured Sax's bass saxophone in one of his choral concerts.*

1846: *Sax received the patent for making saxophones, covering 14 different versions of the original design.*

1850: *The saxophone became popular in French military bands.*

1866: *Sax's patent expired and other instrument makers adapted Sax's original, adding extra keys.*

1920: *The bass saxophone became very common in many jazz music recordings from this period.*

1940s onwards: *The saxophone became associated with swing and big band music.*

Saxophone range

Two and a half octaves

Top saxophonists

Jazz music has produced many impressive saxophone players. **John Coltrane** was a tenor saxophonist, composer, and band leader who had a huge influence on jazz music in the 1960s and 1970s. **Stan Getz**, earned his nickname "The Sound" because of his warm, perfectly controlled saxophone sound and **Sidney Bechet** was a child prodigy in New Orleans. The sax players **Charlie Parker** and the UK's **Courtney Pine** have also had a huge influence on the development of jazz.

John Coltrane (1926–1967)

Soprano   Alto   Tenor   Baritone   Bass

Little to large

Adolphe Sax designed 14 different saxophones, which were divided into **seven** different types: sopranino, soprano, alto, tenor, baritone, bass, and contrabass. Those pitched in F and C were meant for orchestral use and those in E flat and B flat were for bands. They all have the **same keys** in the same place, so once you can play one, you should be able to play them all!

LISTEN TO TRACK 30

A solo alto saxophone plays this laid-back blues music. Listen for the syncopation when the player plays a note on an off-beat, which makes the tune more interesting.

Players support the reed against their bottom lip and blow across it into the mouthpiece while fingering the keys that cover the 20 to 23 toneholes along the saxophone's length.

Usually made of natural cane, a **reed** is placed in the mouthpiece. When a player blows into the mouthpiece, the reed vibrates. Wetting the reed before playing helps it to vibrate correctly. Plastic reeds are available, but some players think they are not so good.

Left-hand keys and buttons

Bell brace

Bell

Main body (Only the small soprano saxophone does not have the characteristic S-shaped body.)

Blowing in the wind

The way players use their facial muscles and lip shape when blowing into a woodwind instrument is called "embouchure". Once they have mastered the technique, it can be adapted to achieve a number of different **sound effects** from trilling, slurring, and growling through to flutter tongue and notebend. Players can also achieve a note one octave above the one they are playing by adapting the shape of their throat.

Thumb rest is used to support the body.

Right-hand keys and buttons

There are about 20–23 toneholes, including two small speaker holes.

Pad cups cover the toneholes

Bow

97

MUSICIAN PROFILE

Musician's biography
Joaquín **Rodrigo**

1901: *Born in Valencia, Spain, the youngest of 10 children.*

1904: *Aged three, Rodrigo became ill with diphtheria and lost his sight.*

1924: *Aged 23, Rodrigo's first orchestral work,* Juglares, *was performed in Valencia.*

1927: *Rodrigo moved to Paris and studied at the École Normale de Musique under French composer Paul Dukas. He met other composers, including Manuel de Falla.*

1933: *Rodrigo married Turkish pianist Victoria Kamhi.*

1935: *Rodrigo wrote* Sonada de adiós *for piano, in memory of his teacher, Paul Dukas, who died that year.*

1939: *Rodrigo moved back to Spain and settled in Madrid.*

1940: *World premiere of the* Concierto de Aranjuez *took place in Barcelona, Spain. This brought Rodrigo worldwide fame.*

1941: *A daughter, Cecilia, was born on 27 January. She is Rodrigo's only surviving child.*

1963: *Aged 62, Rodrigo was awarded the Légion d'Honneur by the French government.*

1999: *Aged 98, Rodrigo died in Madrid. He is buried in the family vault in the cemetery of Aranjuez.*

Musician's influences

Igor Stravinsky (1882–1971)
Russian composer Stravinsky created new ways to look at rhythm and melody in 20th century music.

Spanish culture
Inspired by the history, poetry, and music of his home, Rodrigo's music echoes with Spanish melody.

Joaquín Rodrigo

"The greatest source of inspiration is hard work."

Rodrigo playing the piano at his home in Madrid, 1975.

Spanish composer Joaquín Rodrigo lived through almost every year of the 20th century. During this time, he composed hundreds of musical pieces for orchestra, piano, and voice. However, he is best known for his **guitar music** (even though he did not play the instrument himself). Rodrigo caught diphtheria when he was three years old. This left him blind. All his musical works are composed in **braille**.

The classical guitar has become increasingly popular as an instrument in an orchestra. Players show considerable technical skill.

A concert guitar
In the early 1900s, the guitar had lost its popularity as a classical instrument. Rodrigo helped to change this view. His pieces for concert guitar and orchestra placed the guitar on the same level as the violin or piano, and **re-established** the guitar as an important part of mainstream classical music.

Concierto de Aranjuez

Rodrigo is probably best known for his haunting guitar-orchestra piece, **Concierto de Aranjuez**. This is inspired by the beautiful gardens at the Palace of Aranjuez and also the tragic death at birth of his first child. The music is filled with **love** and **longing**, and also **fear**, as Rodrigo's beloved wife, Victoria, was gravely ill at the time and he was afraid she would die, too. This piece has inspired and been rearranged by musicians from other musical styles, such as the jazz legend Miles Davis.

Royal Palace of Aranjuez, near Madrid

19th century Spanish and Italian guitarists, such as Fernando Sor (1778–1839), spread the popularity of the guitar across Europe.

Spanish guitar

Braille notation

Andrés Segovia (1893–1987)

It was at the request of fellow Spaniard and classical guitarist Segovia that Rodrigo wrote his second most popular work for guitar and orchestra. This was *Fantasia para un Gentilhombre* (Fantasy for a gentleman). Segovia was the **gentleman** in the title and also the first to perform the piece in 1958.

Writing music

In a room at home, Rodrigo had a piano and a braille machine. He wrote his compositions in **braille**, then dictated them, note by note, to a copyist, often his wife Victoria. Victoria then wrote out each musician's part on music paper. The couple reviewed the music carefully before sending it to the printers.

Rodrigo and his wife Victoria working together at the piano.

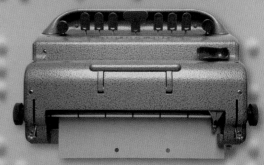

***Braille** machine*

Braille is a way of writing using different patterns of **six raised dots** that blind people can feel with their fingers. The same six dots are used for writing musical notes.

This is D for Dog in braille.

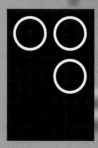

This is also the musical note C.

Recorded sound

His Master's Voice, a picture showing a dog called "Nipper" listening to a gramophone, is an early record label trademark.

In 1877, Thomas Edison made the first recording of a human voice on his newly invented **cylinder phonograph**. This began a wonder of inventions in the recording world, from **gramophone** records to today's fourth generation (4G) technology. The birth of radio provided a springboard for musicians and this continues today with the availability of **digital music downloads**.

On this Edison tin foil phonograph sound is recorded as indentations on foil wrapped around a cylinder.

▶ John McCormack, 1884–1945, Irish

Tenor John McCormack sang classical and popular songs. He made his first recording in 1904 on a **cylinder phonograph**. In the 1910s and 1920s, he recorded for a leading producer of phonograph records, The Victor Talking Machine Company.

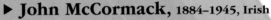

◀ Nora Bayes, 1880–1928, American

A popular singer during World War I, Nora Bayes performed morale-boosting songs for Allied troops. Her song, *Over There*, written in 1917, became an international hit and the **anthem for America's war effort**. Bayes recorded on phonographic records.

Sheet music for Over There, *written by George M. Cohan.*

▼ Bing Crosby, 1903–1977, American

Bing Crosby, one of the most successful recording artists of all time, made the **best-selling record ever**, *White Christmas*. He is famous for his "crooner" sound, developed by singing close to the new-style microphones, introduced by Bell Labs in the USA in 1926.

▼ Benny Goodman, 1909–1986, American

Clarinet player Benny Goodman and his band played a style of jazz that made people dance. Goodman began recording in the 1920s, and then, with his band, went on to take a regular slot in the **nationwide radio programme**, *Let's Dance*.

New style microphone

◄ Smokey Robinson,
1940–, American
In 1960, Smokey Robinson and the Miracles recorded their hit single, *Shop Around*. Their record label was **Motown Records**, founded by an African American, Berry Gordy, and set up to promote African American artists and the soul-pop sound known as Motown.

▼ Jimi Hendrix, 1942–1970, American
Legendary rock guitarist and record producer Jimi Hendrix broke new ground in using the recording studio as an extension of his musical ideas, experimenting with stereophonic and phasing effects. His band, The Jimi Hendrix Experience, recorded its first album on 12 inch vinyl in 1967, which Track Records released as its **first long playing (LP) record.**

Smokey Robinson with Esther Gordy Edwards (Berry's older sister) at the Motown Records office in 1967.

▲ Patsy Cline, 1932–1963, American
The **Grand Ole Opry radio show** began broadcasting country music from Nashville, USA, in 1925. It featured top country artists, including Patsy Cline, who joined the cast in 1961.

► Slim Dusty, 1927–2003,
Australian Slim Dusty wrote and sang country songs about ordinary Australians and life in the bush. His hits included *Waltzing Matilda,* which astronauts Bob Crippen and John Young **broadcast from the space shuttle** Columbia in 1981 when it passed over Australia.

◄ Utada Hikaru,
1983–, Japanese-
American Internet users commonly download digital copies of their favourite songs. In 2007, Japanese artist Utada Hikaru had the **highest selling digital single**, *Flavor of Life,* with more than seven million legal downloads.

Musician's biography
Frank **Sinatra**

1915: *He was born in Hoboken, New Jersey, USA. His father was a fireman, prize-fighter, and bar owner, and his mother was an aspiring politician. They wanted Sinatra to become a civil engineer.*

1935: *Aged 20, formed a band, The Hoboken Four, with some friends and then became a club singer.*

1939: *Married Nancy Barbato with whom he had two daughters, (singer) Nancy and Christina, and a son, Frank Jr.*

1940: *Aged 25, joined Tommy Dorsey's big band as lead singer.*

1942: *Aged 27, he recorded his first solo track. The Frank Sinatra craze began.*

1945: *Starred in* Anchors Away, *a film with Hollywood actor Gene Kelly.*

1953: *Aged 38, Sinatra signed with Capitol records to boost his dwindling music career. He won an Oscar for "Best supporting actor" for his performance in* From Here to Eternity.

1967: *Back to topping the charts, he sang a duet at this time with his daughter Nancy.*

1971: *Aged 56, he announced his retirement, but his fans wouldn't let him (and he didn't really want to!). He continued to appear in films.*

1998: *Aged 83, died of a heart attack in Los Angeles.*

Musician's influences

Bing Crosby (1903–1977)
Sinatra is said to have decided to become a singer after hearing Bing Crosby on the radio.

Billie Holiday (1915–1959)
In the 1940s, Sinatra regularly heard Billie sing in the clubs and learnt from her how to project real emotion into his voice.

Frank Sinatra

Sinatra performed in Las Vegas for more than 40 years.

"Throughout my career, if I have done anything, I have paid attention to every note and every word I sing... If I cannot project this to a listener, I fail."

In Los Angeles, 1943, Sinatra was one of the first singing teen idols.

From the bobby-soxers...

In the early 1950s, Sinatra's teenage fans were called bobby-soxers because they wore poodle skirts (swinging full skirts) and **rolled down** socks. Dances were often held in school gyms with polished wooden floors, so students had to take off their shoes and dance in their socks.

... to the Rat Pack

Later on, in the 1950s and 1960s, Sinatra became known as the leader of the Rat Pack, a group of hard-drinking friends that included, among others, **Dean Martin** and **Sammy Davis Jr**. They used to turn up at each other's concerts to give extra performances, so a billing for a show featuring Dean Martin, would say "Maybe Frank, Maybe Sammy" underneath.

Frank Sinatra was one of the first entertainment **superstars**. His career spanned 60 years and included acting in, directing, and producing over 50 films, as well as singing. His songs have a **timeless**, classic quality and include such hits as *New York, New York* and *My Way*. He won 11 Grammys, three Golden Globes, and two Oscars, as well as many humanitarian awards.

Sinatra is one of the most popular solo artists of all time. He performed on over 1,800 recordings, including over 70 albums and hundreds of singles, and remains as popular as ever.

Famous songs:
Moon River
Come Fly with Me
The Lady is a Tramp
Let it Snow, Let it Snow, Let it Snow
Fly me to the Moon

Famous films:
From Here to Eternity
Guys and Dolls
Meet me in Las Vegas
High Society

All that jazz

By the 1950s, **microphones** were widely used. Using one meant Sinatra could sing softly and with intense emotion, as if telling a story. Sinatra worked very hard at his singing, jogging and swimming underwater to try to increase his lung capacity and learning a sneaky sideways **circular breathing** technique so he could hold a note for ages. His singing style was influenced by jazz and swing but he had a sound all to himself.

Smartly dressed, Sinatra often wore a bow tie and a dinner jacket with a handkerchief in the pocket.

Sinatra gave Marilyn a white poodle puppy, which she called Maf.

A busy love life

Sinatra married four times. Some of his wives and girlfriends were actresses and **celebrities** such as Ava Gardner, Mia Farrow, and Marilyn Monroe. He was well-known for his high-profile love life, and love was a theme that ran through many of his songs.

In 1994, Sinatra was honoured with a Lifetime Achievement Award. At the ceremony, **Bono**, lead singer of the band U2, and Sinatra sang *I've Got You Under My Skin* from *Duets*.

The recording event of the decade

In 1993 and 1994, Sinatra released two new albums – all duets with popular international singers of different musical styles. The music included the Brazilian bossa nova style of **Antônio Carlos Jobim**, the swinging jazz style of **Tony Bennett**, the romantic ballad style of Spanish singer **Julio Iglesias**, and the Cuban soul style of **Jon Secada**. *Duets II* went on to win the Grammy for best album.

Memorable musicals

Musicals are plays that mix music, acting, singing, and dancing. The style developed from the **comic light operettas** of the late 1800s, but in the 1940s and 1950s the plots became more thought-provoking. Around the world there are famous streets or parts of cities where musicals are performed, such as **Broadway** in New York, USA, and London's **West End**.

▲ **Pansori Epic Chant, since 17th century, Korea** In this form of Korean musical theatre, a singer and drummer perform together. While the singer tells a story through songs, stylized speech, and bold gestures, the drummer beats out a musical rhythm. A performance can last up to eight hours.

▲ **Anything Goes, 1934, music and lyrics by Cole Porter** A musical comedy set on board a cruise liner. Passengers include stowaway Billy Crocker, heiress Hope Harcourt, a nightclub singer, a gangster, and an English lord. Billy spends an eventful journey trying to win Hope's heart and songs include the famous *Anything Goes* and *You're the Top*.

▼ **The Threepenny Opera, 1928, music by Kurt Weill and lyrics by Bertolt Brecht** Based on John Gay's, *The Beggar's Opera*, *The Threepenny Opera* isn't really an opera at all. Its story is the tangled lives of a group of beggars, and songs such as *Mack the Knife* were popular hits.

▼ **Peter and the Wolf, 1936, Sergei Prokofiev** A children's story about a boy, Peter, who ventures out into the meadow where he meets a little bird, a duck, a cat – and a dangerous wolf. The story is told by a narrator and each character is played by a different musical instrument.

▼ **The Sound of Music,** 1959, music by Richard Rodgers and lyrics by Oscar Hammerstein II Maria, a young nun, becomes governess for the Austrian von Trapp family. She encourages the children to sing – and falls in love with their father, Captain von Trapp.

▲ **West Side Story,** 1957, music by Leonard Bernstein and lyrics by Stephen Sondheim Based on William Shakespeare's play *Romeo and Juliet*, *West Side Story* is set in New York City in the mid-1950s. Here a girl and boy fall in love. Sadly, they come from different gangs. It ends badly.

◄ **Les Misérables,** 1980, music by Claude-Michel Schönberg, libretto by Alain Boublil, and lyrics by Herbert Kretzmer This unhappy musical is based on an 1862 novel by Victor Hugo. It is set in France at a time of revolution. *Les Misérables* (which means The Miserable Ones) is a global hit and the London production is still running after 25 years.

▼ **Cookin'** *Nanta,* 1997 A Korean comedy show where no one talks, but where drumbeats, magic, and acrobatics dramatize the story. It takes place in a kitchen where a group of chefs are preparing a banquet.

▲ **Phantom of the Opera,** 1986, music by Andrew Lloyd Webber, lyrics by Charles Hart and Richard Stilgoe An opera's lead performer is scared off by a falling backdrop, and so Christine, a young singer, takes her place. Christine has had music lessons from the ghostly phantom of the opera. Although Christine is in love with another, the phantom wants to keep her for himself and steals her away to his lair. This is the most popular and most seen musical ever.

Musician's biography
Elvis **Presley**

1935: *Elvis was born into a poor, working-class family in Mississippi, USA. He was an only child (his twin died at birth).*

1948: *Aged 13, he moved to Memphis, Tennessee, into a mainly African American neighbourhood.*

1954: *Aged 19, he was signed by Sun Records label in Memphis. His first single,* That's All Right, *was a hit.*

1956: *Already an international sensation, aged 21, he starred in his first film,* Love Me Tender.

1958: *Aged 23, drafted into the army to do two years' national service.*

1960–1968: *Elvis starred in a series of films. He made 33 films altogether.*

1967: *Aged 32, married Priscilla Beaulieu, his long-term girlfriend, and had his only child, daughter Lisa-Marie, in 1968.*

1969: *An international superstar, Elvis did a four-week, 57-show engagement in Las Vegas.*

1969–1973: *At his peak, he was fit and energetic on stage, and began wearing his capes and karate suits. He had a gruelling schedule of shows.*

1973–1977: *The shows continued, and increasingly Elvis relied on prescription drugs.*

1977: *Aged 42, Elvis suddenly died of heart failure. Around the world people were shocked by his death.*

Musician's influences

Arthur Crudup (1905–1974)
Delta blues singer and guitarist, Crudup wrote songs used by Elvis.

Rufus Thomas (1917–2001)
Pioneer of American popular music, Thomas was keen to entertain and dedicated to his music.

Elvis Presley

"Music should be something that makes you gotta move, inside or outside."

Elvis Presley, also known as "The King of Rock-and-Roll", or simply **"The King"**, doesn't need much introduction. He is one of the most important figures in popular culture, at the forefront of **rock-and-roll**, and the singer of such hits as *Heartbreak Hotel, Love Me Tender, Jailhouse Rock, Hound Dog*, and many, many more.

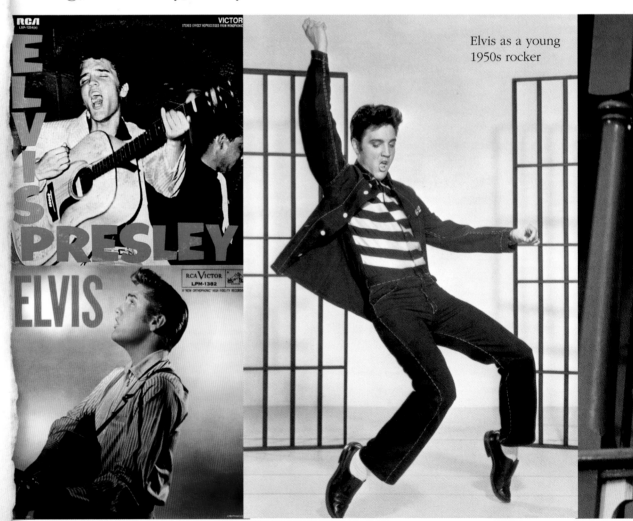

Elvis as a young 1950s rocker

Elvis's looks and moves

Not only was Elvis's sound unique, but also the way he performed. He sent audiences wild by **shaking** his legs and **swivelling** his hips. During the 1950s, he was often censored on television for being too risqué. He was good-looking and charismatic with a great sense of humour, all of which electrified his performances.

Over 1 billion records sold!

Elvis loved the rhythm and blues that was played in the streets around his house, as well as the pop and country music of the time. He also attended African American churches and was heavily influenced by gospel music. He **revolutionized** popular music by fusing these styles into his own unique sound – a mixture of black and white music. From his first hit, it was obvious that Elvis was going places. He is now the **biggest-selling** solo artist of all time, with an estimated over one billion records sold.

Elvis dressed as "The King" in the 1970s, wearing a jewelled karate suit.

Elvis as a 1960s film star

Elvis – the legend

• Elvis is the most impersonated celebrity ever. There are estimated to be over 80,000 people making a living impersonating him.

• Elvis got his first guitar for his 12th birthday.

• Elvis's natural hair colour was sandy blond. (He dyed it black for a film in 1956 and kept it that way.)

• Elvis was a black belt in karate.

• More people (1.5 billion viewers) watched Elvis's *Aloha From Hawaii* concert on TV than watched the first Moon landing (600 million viewers).

• In 1960, just after Elvis left the army, he weighed just over 76 kg (12 stone). When he died, in 1977, he weighed just under 120 kg (19 stone).

• Elvis recorded more than 600 songs in his music career, but wrote or co-wrote only 10 of them.

• Some of Elvis's jewel-encrusted jumpsuits weighed more than 12 kg (2 stone).

A sad end

Elvis's death in 1977 was sadly premature. Violently against drugs and alcohol all his life, Elvis was, however, prescribed drugs to help him sleep and overcome anxiety, and these contributed to a heart attack. His death **shocked** the world. Over 80,000 people lined the processional route from his home in Graceland to the Forest Hill Cemetery. (His remains were later moved back to Graceland after someone tried to steal his body.)

Graceland

Graceland was Elvis's home and has become a **pilgrimage spot** for Elvis's legions of fans. It attracts half a million visitors annually and is the second most visited home in the USA, after the White House.

Musicians' biography
The **Beatles**

1957: *16-year-old John Lennon formed a band called The Quarrymen with school friends, who gradually dropped out to be replaced by 15-year-old Paul McCartney on guitar and, in 1958, by George Harrison on lead guitar (aged just 14).*

1960: *The band renamed themselves The Beatles and played rock-and-roll.*

1962: *Music store manager Brian Epstein became their manager, directing their career until his death in 1967. Original drummer Pete Best was replaced by Ringo Starr for a first recording session at London's Abbey Road Studio. George Martin produced their first hit single, Love Me Do.*

1963: *The Beatles released their first album, Please Please Me.*

1964: *On first US tour greeted with Beatlemania at every port of call.*

1970: *Paul McCartney left "for personal, business, and musical differences" and the Beatles quietly came to an end.*

Musicians' influences

Everly Brothers
Don (1937–) and Phil (1939–) were country-influenced rock-and-roll performers, who sang in close harmony.

Buddy Holly (1936–1959)
Inspired by Elvis Presley, Holly was a pioneer of rock-and-roll music.

The Beatles chose their name partly in homage to Holly's band, The Crickets.

LISTEN TO TRACK 31
Try out some air guitar moves in time with this lively 1960s rock-and-roll piece. Get down low, exaggerate the strumming and picking movements, and kick out a leg as you jump.

The **Beatles**

"There's a lot of random in our songs... writing, thinking, letting others think of bits – then bam, you've the jigsaw puzzle."
Paul McCartney

The Beatles were one of the first boy bands and the best-selling **rock-and-roll group** of all time. From Liverpool, UK, there were four members: John Lennon, Paul McCartney, George Harrison, and Ringo Starr. The **Fab Four's** arrival on the music scene in the 1960s triggered a musical revolution, the perfect accompaniment to the social revolution of the time, which set the kids of the world alight.

Beatlemania

The Beatles inspired a **frenzy** among their teenage fans, especially during the early years of their success. Teenage girls would try to mob them wherever they went, and sometimes they literally had to run to escape.

The Summer of Love

The Beatles' music was played throughout the so-called "Summer of Love", 1967, when **hippie culture** spread around the world. Flower power, communal living, and free love were the hippies' ideology. The Beatles released songs and albums that were perfectly in tune with the times, including *Strawberry Fields Forever* and *Sgt. Pepper's Lonely Hearts Club Band*, as well as their TV show the *Magical Mystery Tour*. But their song that summed up the **mood** most of all was *All You Need Is Love*.

The Beatles and their wives with the Maharishi Mahesh Yogi in India, 1968

With a witty and energetic style, the band performed their crisp harmonies and catchy melodies.

A powerful partnership

John Lennon and Paul McCartney were extraordinary **songwriters** and, between 1962 and 1969, they wrote around 180 jointly credited songs. Many Beatles songs are mostly the work of one or the other but they used each other to bounce ideas off, and often ended up putting some of the other's ideas into their songs. This meant they could be competitive, but also gain **inspiration** from each other. The merging of ideas of these two great talents is often said to be the key reason for the Beatles' huge success.

Discography

Since the release of their first album Please Please Me, *which went straight to the top of the charts in 1963, nearly every single and album they released until 1970 hit the Number 1 spot. Many broke all previously held sales records. These are some of their hits:*

1963 *She Loves You*
1963 *I Want To Hold Your Hand*
1964 *A Hard Day's Night*
1965 *Ticket To Ride*
1965 *Help!*
1965 *We Can Work It Out*
1966 *Eleanor Rigby*
1966 *Paperback Writer*
1967 *All You Need Is Love*
1967 *Hello Goodbye*
1968 *Hey Jude*
1969 *Get Back*

The Yellow Submarine

In 1968, The Beatles released an **animated** musical film called *Yellow Submarine*. When the music-hating Blue Meanies take over Pepperland, a music-loving undersea paradise, they turn the inhabitants into statues. The only survivor, Old Fred, escapes in a yellow submarine and finds The Beatles, who join him on a **bizarre** journey back to Pepperland to restore love and music.

Reggae music

How did it happen?

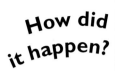

Reggae music, the heartbeat of the newly independent Jamaica, emerged in the 1960s from a mix of **American** and **African** musical styles. With its chanted vocals, bass-guitar-led riffs, and off-beat guitar chords, reggae has brought Jamaican dance music international recognition.

Lord Flea and his Calypsonians

Mento, a mix of European and African folk dance music that began in the 1940s, became the first Jamaican recorded music in 1951.

As people couldn't afford live musicians, travelling disc-jockeys (DJs) entertained at parties on their sound systems, consisting of large speakers, a record-playing deck, and a powerful amplifier. DJs, such as Clement Dodd (shown here) and Duke Reid, would spin the records and add rhyming vocals over the music known as **"toasting"**.

SOUND SYSTEMS

Many Rastafarians choose to wear their hair in dreadlocks, which are formed by not combing or cutting the hair.

A growing movement in Jamaica since the 1930s, Rastafari is a faith based on following a way of life celebrating their African roots. By the late 1960s, the ideas of this movement were to inspire the lyrics of **roots reggae** musicians.

RASTAFARIANS

The Skatalites

By the beginning of the 1960s, Jamaican R&B, jazz riffs, and mento music had merged to form a distinct style known as **ska**, with its dominant bass and emphasis on the off-beats.

SKA

In 1966, soul music was merged with ska to create a much slower music with a more refined harmony known as **rocksteady**. Lyrics were about the social unrest of the time and electric instruments were used.

ROCKSTEADY

Reggae lyrics were sung in Jamaican patois – a mix of Creole English, African, Portuguese, Spanish, and Rasta slang.

LISTEN TO TRACK 32

Dance along to this catchy reggae song: set your feet about 30 cm (12 in) apart, slightly bend your knees, relax your body, and "wind" your hips in a S-shape – as right hip rises, left hip drops. Make up your own arm moves.

In 1962, Jamaica became a country independent from British rule, but there was increasing unrest in the ghettos (poor areas) due to the many social problems. Dressed like "mods", disheartened youths needed a voice and developed their own vocal style of ska known as **rude boy** music.

By the late 1960s, music studios in Jamaica had been improved, making possible a change from rocksteady music to reggae. **Reggae** music featured an African nyah-bingi hand-drumming style making a heartbeat rhythm, tricky lead-bass arrangement, off-beat guitar chords known as **skank**, and lyrics sung in Jamaican patois.

REGGAE

Since the late 1960s, reggae music has inspired musicians both from Jamaica and from other countries...

Jamaican musicians

Promoting reggae
In 1972, the Jamaican crime film *The Harder They Come* starred the reggae singer Jimmy Cliff in the lead role, and also included on its **soundtrack** reggae music from The Melodians, Desmond Dekker, The Maytals, The Slickers, and Scotty. The film helped to introduce reggae music to the USA and Europe.

Bob Marley (1945–1981)
The international popularity of Marley, the lead singer of The Wailers (formed in 1964), gave reggae and the Rastafarian movement **worldwide recognition**.

Abyssinians (formed 1968)
This roots reggae band sang in close harmony. Their first song *Satta Massagana*, released in 1971, was a **Rastafarian hymn,** part of which is sung in the ancient Ethiopian Amharic language.

Lee "Scratch" Perry (1936–)
This reggae musician and producer became one of the creators of **dub music** – remixing a record by removing the vocal part, using the bass and drum textures, and creating special effects in a recording studio.

Sly Dunbar and Robbie Shakespeare (formed 1975)
Meeting in the reggae band The Revolutionaries, Sly on drums and Robbie on bass guitar have been influential in creating new sounds, such as the harder beat known as **"Rockers"** and the **"rub-a-dub"** sound.

Judy Mowatt (1952–)
One of the **first female** reggae performers and producers, Mowatt worked with the singer Freddie McGregor to co-produce *Black Woman* in 1978.

Outside Jamaica

UB40 (formed 1978)
This **British reggae band** released the song *Red Red Wine* in 1983 (originally recorded by ballad singer Neil Diamond in 1967 and then by Jamaican reggae singer Tony Tribe in 1969), which stayed in the charts for over a hundred weeks.

Men at Work (formed 1979)
In 1981, this **Australian rock band** influenced by reggae music released the single *Down Under*, which became an instant hit.

Matisyahu (1979–)
This American musician combines a **Jewish traditional musical** style with background reggae music as well as rock and hip hop sounds.

Electric **guitar**

Electric guitars in history

1920s: *Jazz guitarists started looking for ways to make their guitars louder.*

1930s: *The first electric guitar was the "Frying Pan", made by George Beauchamp in 1931.*

The Vivi-Tone company built the first Spanish-style electric guitar in 1933.

1940s: *The development of electrical amplification meant that electric guitars didn't have to be hollow.*

In 1941, jazz and country guitarist Les Paul built "the Log" from a solid wooden post. Later, he stuck on two halves of an acoustic guitar to improve its looks.

The "Frying Pan"

Leo Fender designed the Fender Esquire in 1949. The solid Spanish-style guitar was a big hit with country, blues, and rock-and-roll musicians.

1950s: *Seeing Fender's success, the Gibson guitar company looked at Les Paul's early designs and released the "Les Paul Standard" in 1952.*

The "log"

Les Paul (1915–2009)

Electric guitar range

Electric guitars normally have a 4-octave range, but this can be extended by adding extra strings. The electric bass guitar has a 3-octave range.

"Sometimes you want to give up the guitar, you'll hate the guitar. But if you stick with it, you're gonna be rewarded." Jimi Hendrix

The invention of the electric guitar was a **breakthrough** in the development of music from the late 1940s onwards – including the blues, rock-and-roll, and heavy metal – and is responsible for the creation of modern popular music as we know it today. Guitars could now be heard over the other instruments in a band and became the **lead instrument.**

*The **bridge** holds the strings in place on the guitar body.*

Pick-ups *translate the vibrations of the strings into an electric current.*

*The **pick-up switch** selects different pick-ups and changes the sound.*

*The **body** of the guitar is usually made from wood.*

Control dials *change the volume and tone produced.*

Amplifier

The guitar is connected to the amplifer by a cable. Here electric signals from the guitar are converted into sound.

Plectrums or plucking

Electric guitars are played by finger-plucking, or by striking the strings with a plectrum, or pick. Picks are small triangular pieces of plastic, although sometimes guitarists may use coins, or bits of glass or stone, instead.

*The **machine heads** are used to tune the strings.*

*The **fretboard** is the surface of the neck beneath the strings.*

Headstock

*The **nut** is the band between the neck and the headstock.*

Neck

Top guitarists

The great guitarists have all developed their own distinctive style and sound. **Jimi Hendrix** (above) was left-handed but played a right-handed guitar, holding it upside down. **Neil Young** uses various pedal effects to get his trademark sound, while **Jimmy Page** sometimes uses a violin bow with his guitar.

*The **frets** are strips of metal inserted at precise points along the neck.*

Fender Stratocaster

Gibson Explorer

Gibson SG

LISTEN TO TRACK 33

Listen for the guitar riffs (clusters or sequences of notes or chords) in this head-banging rock music.

Steve Vai

Guitar virtuoso Steve Vai has played some of the best electric guitar solos ever created, and has inspired many of the top guitarists. An extremely **technically advanced** musician, he has unusually long, and very quick, fingers. Vai has played both the double- and triple-necked guitars. He has a flashy playing style – at one concert he played the guitar with his tongue!

Other guitar types

Electric guitars are now made in many different shapes and materials. They are usually made of wood or plyboard but can also be made of plastic, metal, or even cardboard.

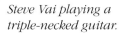

Steve Vai playing a triple-necked guitar.

113

Musicians' biography
Led **Zeppelin**

1968: *Formed as The New Yardbirds but renamed later that year.*

1971: *After three years, the track* Stairway to Heaven *appeared on their fourth album. Although never released as a single, it remains even today one of the most requested songs on the radio.*

1974: *After six years, formed their own record label, Swan Song.*

1980: *After 12 years, their final live concert was on the 7th July in Berlin, Germany.*

1980: *John Bonham died in September, and Led Zeppelin officially disbanded in December.*

Since then, *the band has reformed (with guest drummers including Bonham's son, Jason) to perform charity concerts. Jimmy Page and Robert Plant have had successful solo careers, playing all kinds of music from heavy metal to blues and country.*

Musicians' influences

Roy Harper (1941–)
English folk and rock singer and guitarist, since the mid-1960s and known for his lengthy and intricate finger plucking guitar playing.

Led **Zeppelin**

"One of the most innovative, powerful, and influential groups in rock history." Atlantic Records – Led Zeppelin's American record company

John Paul Jones *(1946–) played the bass guitar, but at times also the mandolin and keyboards.*

Robert Plant *(1948–) was the lead vocalist and lyric-writer from 1969. He often mimicked Page's guitar effects.*

Led Zeppelin warming up for a concert in Minneapolis, USA, in 1975.

Heavy metal music

Loud, aggressive, brash – heavy metal is a form of rock music that emphasizes **rough sound**. Electric guitars are the main heavy metal instruments, and many metal tracks include long guitar solos. Vocals are quite often shouted, and a thumping drum completes the sound.

Jimmy Page, Robert Plant, John Paul Jones, and John Bonham were **Led Zeppelin**, the British band that has been credited with pioneering **heavy metal music**. Led Zeppelin's guitar-led sound has spread all over the world, influencing many other bands. Their second album has been called **"the blueprint of heavy metal"** – yet the band themselves were influenced by all sorts of other music, from classical to folk to reggae.

John Bonham (1948–1980) was the hard-hitting drummer. He used the longest and heaviest drumsticks available.

Jimmy Page playing his Gibson EDS-1275 double-necked guitar.

Jimmy Page (1944–) was the lead guitarist and founder of the band. He inspired many future rock guitarists.

Mixed style

Their albums not only feature the thunderous sounds of heavy metal but also a variety of styles, including acoustic (non-electric or "unplugged") music.

The album with no name

Led Zeppelin's fourth album has **no name**, just a set of four symbols (which represent the band members). After being criticized in the press as over-hyped, the band set out to prove that their music would sell even if no one could tell who made the album. They were right: this is one of the **biggest-selling** albums in music history.

Led Zeppelin

When forming the band, the story goes that on hearing the demo recording, Keith Moon and John Entwistle from the band **The Who** thought it sounded so bad that they told Jimmy Page that they'd go down like a **lead balloon**. A Zeppelin was a 20th century airship.

Discography

Led Zeppelin made nine studio albums, which have sold 200 million copies across the world. They didn't want to release singles, preferring their fans to listen to a whole album, although Atlantic Records did issue 10 album tracks as singles in the USA.

1969 *Led Zeppelin, Led Zeppelin II*
1970 *Led Zeppelin III*
1971 *The fourth album, untitled*
1973 *Houses of the Holy*
1975 *Physical Graffiti (double album)*
1976 *Presence*
1978 *In Through the Out Door*
1982 *Coda*
2007 *Mothership (compilation album)*

Popular music

With the growth of the **youth market** and media developments, pop stars and bands have been launched into hugely successful recording careers. From folk rock to hard rock, soul to disco, some popular music styles have come and gone, while others continue to develop.

How did it happen?

Pop stars were able to become better known by reaching a wider audience through the creation of 45 rpm (revolutions per minute) records for singles in the 1940s, and appearing on television and in films. The popular **music charts** began in the 1950s.

Between 1885 and 1930, music publishers and songwriters based in New York and known as **Tin Pan Alley** recorded and wrote songs that would sell well, such as sentimental ballads, novelty songs, cakewalk and ragtime music, jazz, and blues. This was the beginning of the American music industry.

In 1927, the yodelling singer, Jimmie Rodgers, known as the "Father of country music", became one of the first popular music stars.

Jimmie RODGERS (1897–1933)

Appealing to the **youth culture** of the 1960s, pop stars and bands, such as Elvis Presley and the Beach Boys from the USA, The Beatles and the Rolling Stones from Britain, and The Seekers from Australia (shown above) achieved international chart success.

The Monkees (1966–1970)

Lonnie Donegan Skiffle Group

After World War II, there was a huge baby boom because American servicemen returning home started having families. So suddenly, in the 1960s, there was a huge generation of young people to appeal to, who became known as "teenagers".

Musicians merged folk and rock music in the mid-1960s. Bob Dylan wrote **protest songs**, such as *Blowin' in the Wind*. Canadian singer-songwriter, Leonard Cohen was influenced by European folk music and, in Brazil, Caetano Veloso and Gilberto Gil combined the Bahia folk music with pop and **bossa nova** sound, creating a music style known as *Tropicália*.

Leonard Cohen (1934–)

Music producers began creating pop bands from scratch, choosing members by their looks and their appeal to pre-teens and teenagers. They then went on to **create bands** for cartoon shows and marketing of products like cereals and sweets. These were the forerunners to the created bands of today, such as the Spice Girls.

BUBBLEGUM pop (1967–1972)

Since the 1970s, pop stars have experimented with a mixture of music and dance styles and fashions...

Solo artists

Aretha Franklin (1942–)
Influenced by gospel music, Franklin is known as the **"Queen of Soul"**, enjoying pop success since the late 1960s.

Joni Mitchell (1943–)
In the 1970s, the experimental Canadian singer influenced the **folk rock** movement, writing powerful songs such as *Big Yellow Taxi* (1970).

Sezen Aksu (1954-)
Since the release of her first single in 1975, Aksu has influenced the sound and style of Turkish pop music and is known as the **"Queen of Turkish Pop"**.

Celine Dion (1968-)
This French-Canadian singer has received international recognition since the 1980s for her **large vocal range**. Her biggest hit is *My Heart Will Go On*, the theme song of the 1997 blockbuster film *Titanic*.

Michael Jackson (1958–2009)
Known as the **"King of Pop"**, Jackson began his solo career in 1971. He transformed the use of **music videos** to promote albums. *Thriller* (1982) is the best-selling album of all time.

Herbert Grönemeyer (1956–)
This German rock musician and actor had a breakthrough with his fifth album *4630 Bochum* (1984), which is the **biggest-selling German-language LP**.

Bands

Scorpions (1965–)
Famous since the 1980s, this German **heavy metal hard rock** band has achieved international success with albums such as *Love at First Sting* (1984).

Abba (1972–1982)
The catchy songs and 1970s style of this Swedish **disco pop band** continue to be popular in films and musicals, such as *Mamma Mia!*.

Midnight Oil (1976–2002, reunited 2009)
This Australian **hard rock** band became known for its dramatic live performances and outspoken songs about political causes.

Adventurous **Afropop**

Afropop is the general term to describe African popular music from the mid-20th century onwards. A wide range of styles has emerged across the continent, combining each country's traditional music with American, Latin American, and European influences. The results have been **inspiring**.

◀ **Fela Kuti,** **1938–1997,** **Nigeria** During the 1970s, Kuti was a pioneer of Afrobeat music, which fused West African chants and Yoruba drumming rhythms with jazz and funk rhythms played on horns and multiple guitars.

▲ **Soukous dancer,** **performed 2008,** **Kenya** The soukous dancing craze began in the Congo during the 1930s. Known today as the Congo rumba or lingala, this is a fast, up-beat musical style inspired by Congo traditional music and Cuban and Latin dances.

▲ **Manu Dibango,** **1933–,** **Cameroon** The saxophonist and vibraphone player Dibango developed a musical style known as makossa, which fuses traditional Duala tribe dance with jazz and Latin American music.

▶ **Amadou Bagayoko**, 1954–, **and Mariam Doumbia**, 1958–, **Mali** After meeting at Mali's Institute for the Young Blind, Amadou and Mariam became a musical duo. Their music, known as Afro-blues, mixes traditional Mali sound with international multi-cultural sounds, using instruments such as Syrian violins and tablas.

▼ **Etran Finatawa**, formed 2004, **Niger** The five members of this band come from two neighbouring tribes, the Tuareg and Wodaabe. The band has cleverly combined the two tribes' music to produce a hypnotic musical style known as the nomad blues.

▲ **Thomas Mapfumo**, 1945–, **Zimbabwe** Mapfumo created the popular chimurenga music, which is based on the traditional Shona mbira music (see page 21) now played on electric instruments and containing lyrics about Zimbabwe's social and political struggle.

▶ **N'Faly Kouyaté**, active from the 1990s, **Guinea** Born into a respected family of Mandinka griots (see page 20), Kouyaté is known as the "Jimi Hendrix of the kora". He works with the band Afro Celt Sound System and his own group Dunyakan, giving griot music new vibrancy.

▲ **Youssou N'Dour**, 1959–, **Senegal** N'Dour popularized mbalax music, which is a rhythmic dance combining Afro-Cuban music, jazz, funk, rock, and French pop with traditional Wolof-singing sabar drummers and griots (see page 20).

▶ **Kabelo Mabalane**, 1976–, **South Africa** As a member of TKZee, Kabelo performs kwaito music, which originated in South Africa and is house music combined with African percussion sounds and shouted or chanted lyrics.

119

Hip hop

Hip hop is a rhythmic, vocal style of music associated with rap. It began in the Bronx area of New York City in the 1970s. Set against a background of **beats** sampled from other songs, the performer speaks rather than sings the lyrics. Sometimes the lyrics are pre-written poetry, but some performers prefer to improvise their rhymes to fit the mood of the performance.

How did it happen?

DJ Kool Herc

Hip hop grew out of **block parties** in immigrant communities that featured funk, soul, and disco music. DJs like Kool Herc used the turntable to create **beats** that could be rapped over.

1520, Sedgwick Avenue

The Bronx, New York City

Many street events took place on public basketball courts or at venues like 1520 Sedgwick Avenue in the Bronx. Organizers would **tap into power supplies** to connect their equipment.

Grandmaster Flash and the Furious Five

The term *hip hop* was coined by Keith Cowboy Wiggins, a rapper with Grandmaster Flash. His friend had joined the army and he teased him about the "hip hop" marching rhythm.

Practising moves on the sidewalk

A new style of dancing evolved as hip hop developed. "Breaking" is street slang for "getting excited" or "acting energetically" and this became part of dancing to hip hop.

BREAKDANCING

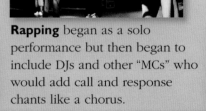

Rapping began as a solo performance but then began to include DJs and other "MCs" who would add call and response chants like a chorus.

RAPPING

The breakbeat technique involves cutting and scratching – moving a record backwards and forwards as it goes round.

Grandmaster Flash

SCRATCHING

Die Fantastischen Vier

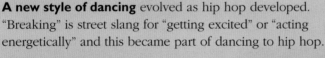

Beatboxing is another vocal technique used in hip hop. Performers **imitate percussion instruments** and other beat noises using their mouth, lips, tongue, and voice.

Hip hop has influenced more than just music – it has a culture all of its own...

DJing

Scratching
This technique uses two turntables and an audio mixer. Sometimes the DJ moves the record back and forth under the needle to create a distinctive **scratchy percussive** sound to go along with a rhythmic beat track.

Sampling
Digital technology enabled DJs to try new techniques. Sections of songs could be sampled and combined into programmable **loops** of sound. Legal issues have led to a decline in use of samples.

LISTEN TO TRACK 34
This is a laid back urban-style hip hop beat, featuring scratching and sampling. Try saying the words of a favourite poem or a nursery rhyme as a rap over the top of this backing track.

Graffiti

Tagging
Graffiti is as much a part of hip hop as dancing and rapping. It took off in New York in the 1960s as small, **localized tags** of the artist's name, but soon spread to large public sites as graffiti artists started competing against rival crews for attention and recognition.

Graffiti art
As new forms of spray paint and marker pens became available, tags became more **artistic**. Trains were often targeted, as these moved around the cities and showed the artist's work to a wider audience.

ANOTHER DIRECTION

Looking the part
Hip hop fans have their own style of urban clothing: baggy trousers, athletic or hooded jackets, tee-shirt, and often a back-to-front baseball cap. As more money poured into the music it gained a "bling" aspect, with flashy jewellery and **designer accessories**. Breakdancers prefer trainers or sneakers that give them a good grip and flexibility. Bandannas and caps help with headspins, and wristbands are often placed along arms to reduce friction and for protection.

Breakdance

Street dancing
Breakdancing is known as "b-boying" (or "b-girling") or "breaking" to those who perform it. It is a mixture of dance and **acrobatics** with moves that include popping, spinning, and freezing.

Battles
Part of hip hop culture involves "battles" between different dancers who try to **out-dance** each other. They often do it to settle disputes, going on until one of them admits defeat.

ELECTRO

Recording
Most early hip hop took the form of live performances by DJs at **block parties**. Early recordings show how much hip hop has changed since those days.

Television and film music

Since the invention of film and television, music has been an essential part of the opening and closing credits of programmes and films. Music is also used to accompany the drama, **creating moods** such as calm or tension. In advertisements, catchy **jingles** help to sell products. Composers are often chosen for their particular musical style.

▲ **Black Orpheus,** 1959, **music by Antônio Carlos Jobim and Luis Bonfá** This tragic love story is set in Rio de Janeiro, Brazil. It's carnival time, and jazz and lively Brazilian samba rhythms merge with the sounds of the street.

▲ **Goodbye Mary Poppins,** 1983, **Maksim Dunayevsky** Based on Mary Poppins, the mysterious flying nanny made famous by Julie Andrews in the 1964 Disney film version, this is a two-part Russian musical TV miniseries. Its music is in the style of 1970s and 1980s film music.

◄ **Antarctica,** 1991, **Nigel Westlake** This is a documentary film about the world's coldest continent, Antarctica. There, humans work on research stations, while penguins and seals live their lives on the ice. Australian Nigel Westlake has written music that reflects the landscape and ties in so closely with the movements of the animals that at times they look as though they are dancing to the music.

▲ **Instruments of the Orchestra,** 1946, **Benjamin Britten** British composer Benjamin Britten wrote *Young Person's Guide to the Orchestra* for an educational documentary film called *The Instruments of the Orchestra*. Britten sub-titled the work *Variations and Fugue on a Theme of Purcell*. The same music is repeated by different sections of the orchestra, such as wind or percussion instruments, so that children can learn the sounds they make. It ends with all the instruments playing the tune together in a loud, uplifting finale.

▲ The Simpsons Theme, 1989,

Danny Elfman The music for this popular TV show has a retro style reminiscent of TV shows from the 1960s. Different arrangements of the same piece are used to tie in with the length of the opening cartoon sequence.

▲ Crouching Tiger, Hidden

Dragon, 2000, **Tan Dun** The film score for this magical martial arts film is a mix of Eastern and Western musical styles. Asian instrumentals, pop, and cello solos by Yo-Yo Ma work alongside each other to reflect the ancient Chinese scenery and the characters' emotions.

▲ Central Station, 1998, Jaques

Morelenbaum and Antonio Pinto

Set in Brazil, this is the story of the friendship between a middle-aged woman and a young boy. The award-winning music is full of emotion, like the story, and has reduced audiences to tears.

▲ Star Wars, 1977–2005, John Williams

American John Williams wrote the film score for the six Star Wars films. Much of the music is active, with a quick tempo, and helps to build the tension of the story. Williams's music also expresses and emphasizes the emotions of the characters.

▲ Advertising jingles for Turkey Tourism Campaign,

2000–2002, Fahir Atakoglu As well as writing music for films and documentaries, Turkish composer and pianist Fahir Atakoglu has used his skill as a jingle writer to convey an immediate message in his music.

123

MUSICIAN PROFILE

Musician's biography
A. R. **Rahman**

1966: *Born in Tamil Nadu, India, he was named A. S. Dileep Kumar, the second of four children.*

1975: *Aged nine, his father died. His father, R. K. Shekhar, was a composer and conductor.*

1977: *Aged 11, he began to play keyboard professionally to help support his family.*

1987: *Aged 21, he began recording advertising jingles.*

c. 1988: *One of his sisters became very ill. As the family believed a Muslim spiritual leader made her well again, they converted to Islam. He adopted his new name, Allah Rakha Rahman.*

1992: *Rahman's first soundtrack for the film* Roja (Rose) *won an award for Best Music Director at the National Film Awards.*

2001: *Aged 35, Rahman worked with British composer Andrew Lloyd Webber on his stage musical,* Bombay Dreams, *which opened in London's West End in 2002. This ran for two years before transferring briefly to Broadway in New York, USA.*

2008: *Aged 42, Rahman composed the soundtrack to* Slumdog Millionaire.

Musician's influences

Tamil music
Tamil music has evolved from the Carnatic music of southern India (see page 32).

Jim Reeves (1923–1964)
Among the first Western musicians Rahman heard was Jim Reeves, an American country and pop singer and songwriter.

A. R. **Rahman**

"I do believe in a universal music because all of us are, in a way, getting multicultural…"

Scene from the musical Bombay Dreams, 2002

Rahman's studio
Rahman composes in his high-tech recording studio in Chennai, India's entertainment capital. First he watches the film and then works out the music using his own voice and a piano. Later, he **records** professional singers and instrumentalists and then edits the recordings, putting together the best parts to make the final, polished piece.

The music of this Indian **award-winning** film composer and record producer is a mix of different styles, from traditional Indian to Western classical, reggae, rock, and jazz. In 2008, Rahman wrote the music for the hit film, *Slumdog Millionaire*. This brought him to the attention of a **worldwide** audience and made him a global star.

Like Rahman, M.I.A. borrows from different types of music, from Brazilian electro-rap and Bollywood vocals to Aboriginal rap and disco.

In 2009, Rahman received two Academy Awards (Oscars) for best original score and best original song for *Slumdog Millionaire*.

Awards and accolades

Rahman is a **prolific composer**, often working on six films at a time. His awards include 14 Filmfare Awards and four National Film Awards in India, a BAFTA Award in the UK, and a Golden Globe, two Grammy Awards, and two Oscars in the USA. In 2010, he received the Padma Bhushan from the President of India – an award for distinguished services to his country.

M.I.A. (1975–)

Rahman co-wrote *O Saya* for *Slumdog Millionaire* with Sri Lankan-British rapper M.I.A. This music is a mixture of **Bollywood** and **hip hop** and sets the scene for the film: edgy, urban, and loud.

Once upon a time in India
Rahman has written more than 130 film scores for Bollywood, the Hindi-language Indian film industry. **Bollywood films** are usually lavish musicals, filled with melodrama, romance, comedy, and daredevil thrills.

Rahman's soundtrack for *Lagaan*, a Bollywood film released in 2001, was a mix of Indian classical music, folk tunes, and jazz.

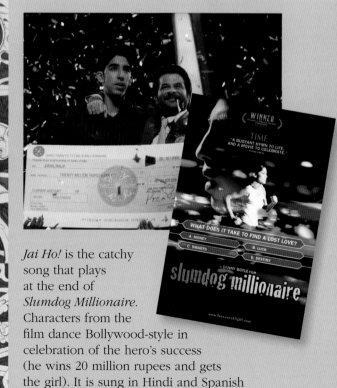

Jai Ho! is the catchy song that plays at the end of *Slumdog Millionaire*. Characters from the film dance Bollywood-style in celebration of the hero's success (he wins 20 million rupees and gets the girl). It is sung in Hindi and Spanish and won the Academy Award for Best Original Song in 2009.

Classical (1970s–)

Modern classical music has taken many different directions, splitting into varied styles. Composers have experimented with harmonies, melodies, and rhythms, sometimes combining many at the same time or removing them completely. The use of **electronic** instruments and computer **technology** has also opened up musical possibilities.

How did it happen?

Hindemith **modernized** music in an inventive and witty way by mixing the 1920s jazz style with classical forms and Bach-style baroque music.

Paul HINDEMITH (1895–1963)

Schoenberg broke new ground with his atonal music (see page 88).

The Rite of Spring, *1913, Igor Stravinsky.*

Igor Stravinsky, Charles Ives, and Bela Bartók developed **polytonal** music where different parts played at the same time in different keys.

Shostakovitch was criticized for composing **"discordant** and **confused"** music. He combined different trends: tonal with atonal music, and romantic with violent emotion.

Dmitri SHOSTAKOVITCH (1906–1975)

The Australian composer Grainger pioneered the idea of **"free music"** experimenting with random, gliding music where there's no set rhythm or pitch. He devised elastic scoring, meaning that a work could be played by any instruments.

Percy GRAINGER (1882–1961)

The French composer Messiaen featured an early electronic instrument, the **ondes martenot** with its trembling swooping sound, in his *Turangalîla-Symphonie* in 1948.

Olivier MESSIAEN (1908–1992)

Cage developed the idea of music happening by chance. He created *4'33"*, a piece of silence where any **"chance"** noises during its performance became part of the work.

John CAGE (1912–1992)

Ligeti devised a pictorial method, or graphic score, for notating sounds.

In the 1950s and 1960s, composers such as **Karlheinz Stockhausen** broke new ground in electronic music, manipulating the playback of tape recordings through loudspeakers. In Hungary, **György Ligeti** experimented with creating a new shifting orchestral sound without a clear melody.

IRCAM (Institut de Recherche et Coordination Acoustique/Musique) building in Paris.

In the 1970s, the French composer **Pierre Boulez** founded an institution for music research and experimentation, IRCAM. The Greek composer **Iannis Xenakis,** who was interested in the mathematics of music, also used **computer programmes** to create compositions.

In 1964, the American **Terry Riley** composed *In C*, where any number of instrumentalists repeated a short phrase over and over at different times before moving on to the next phrase at some point. Other composers, such as **Philip Glass** and **La Monte Young** developed this slowly shifting **minimalist** music.

Since the 1970s, classical composers continue to be experimental...

National music

Luciano Berio (1925–2003)

Working at IRCAM in the 1970s, Berio studied **speech patterns** and applied this to music. His compositions are also inspired by Sicilian folk music.

Tõru Takemitsu (1930–1996)

Takemitsu combines traditional **Japanese scales** and instruments with Western styles and orchestra, creating interesting harmonies.

Sir Peter Maxwell Davies (1934–)

Inspired by the Scottish Orkney landscape, Davies's music is very **theatrical** and uses vocal and dramatic effects. He is currently Master of the Queen's Music in the UK.

Minimalists

Arvo Pärt (1935–)

The Estonian composer Pärt experiments with minimalist orchestral techniques to convey **poetic** sounds in his religious music.

Steve Reich (1936–)

Inspired by tape-loops and speech recordings, Reich creates rippling, **phase-shifting** music where the instruments steadily play at slightly different speeds.

John Adams (1947–)

Adams applies a lively sense of humour and **rhythmic excitement** to minimalism, and writes pieces based on world headlines and major historical events.

New directions

Kevin Volans (1949–)

After working with Stockhausen, this South African composer has combined **African sounds** and techniques with his own style.

Kaija Saariaho (1952–)

This Finnish composer experiments with a combination of **synthesized** electronic and instrumental sounds to produce dramatic and mysterious new music.

Mark-Anthony Turnage (1960–)

Blood on the Floor (1996) by Turnage is typical of his handling of contemporary subjects with **jazz elements** and a dramatic, aggressive style in his music.

Live music

Every night in towns and cities around the world, musicians perform live in all sorts of **venues** – on street corners and in parks, in small clubs and beautiful concert halls, and in vast sports arenas for classical and pop concerts. Music can be performed almost anywhere and for any occasion or reason. Live music brings performer and audience together in a **shared experience** of feelings and emotions.

▶ **Tribute concert, Lisbon, Portugal** In her long career, Portuguese singer Amália Rodrigues spread the popularity of fado, a longing, mournful-sounding Portuguese urban folk music. Amália was much loved, both at home and abroad. These singers are performing a tribute concert at the opening of the Fado Museum after Amália's death.

▼ **Champs de Mars, Paris, France**
Some concerts are held in celebration of big sporting events. In 1998, the Three Tenors performed a concert in Paris ahead of the World Cup Football final. The three superstars of opera; Plácido Domingo, José Carreras, and Luciano Pavarotti, sang in front of the Eiffel Tower and fireworks exploded into the sky.

◄ Barbican Centre,
London, UK In 2009, the jazz
group Portico Quartet performed
at the Barbican Centre. Many bands
and musicians perform at arts
centres, theatres, clubs, and pubs.
These live gigs are a great way to
get to know new artists and
explore different musical styles.

◄ Canecão, Rio de Janeiro,
Brazil Chico Buarque has performed
regularly at the Canecão, a brewery
and beer house in Rio de Janeiro. The
name Canecão means "big mug" in
Portuguese. Over the years, many
great Brazilian and international
musicians have played at this
famous music venue.

◄ Live Earth, London, UK
Madonna performed on stage at
Wembley Stadium for the London
Live Earth concert in 2007. Over
150 musical acts took part in
11 concerts to raise awareness
about climate change. The
concerts were held
simultaneously over seven
continents and were broadcast
in over 130 countries.

▼ Nobel Peace Prize Concert,
Oslo, Norway The Nobel Peace Prize Concert,
which started in 1994, is held every year in honour
of the recipient of the prestigious Nobel Peace
Prize. In 2000, the soprano Sumi Jo was among
those performing in honour of the Nobel Peace
Prize winner Kim Dae-jung.

▲ Eurovision Song Contest,
Riga, Latvia The popular music competition was
created in 1956 to bring the countries of war-torn
Europe together. In the years since its creation, the
competition has expanded to include several
non-European countries. In 2003, the competition
was held in Latvia where the Turkish entry won,
performed by pop singer Sertab Erener.

▲ Musikverein, Vienna, Austria
The Vienna Philharmonic Orchestra is shown
here performing in the golden concert hall of the
Musikverein in Vienna. The orchestra's famous
New Year's Concert has taken place every year
since 1939. The concert always features music
composed by the Strauss family and other
celebrated Austrian composers.

129

Musician's biography
Peter **Sculthorpe**

1929: *Born on 29 April in Launceston, Tasmania, Australia.*

1938: *Aged nine, Sculthorpe started to learn the piano and began composing.*

1955: Sonatina for Piano *premiered at the International Society for Contemporary Music (ISCM) festival in Germany. This brought Sculthorpe international attention.*

1961: *Aged 32, Sculthorpe wrote* Irkanda I, *the first of his Irkanda series on the Australian outback.*

1963: *Sculthorpe began teaching at the University of Sydney.*

1966: *Commissioned to write* Sun Music I, *first of his* Sun Music *series.*

1977: *Aged 48, he wrote one of his best-known works,* Port Essington.

1986: *Wrote* Earth Cry, *about environmental damage and native Australians who had lost their lands.*

2004: *While in his 70s,* Requiem *premiered in Adelaide, Australia.*

Musician's influences

Asian music
Asian music, particularly the sounds of Bali, can be heard in Sculthorpe's work.

Aboriginal music
Aboriginal chanting forms part of Sculthorpe's later works, such as Requiem *(2004).*

Peter Sculthorpe

"It always seems foolish not to take heed of a music that has been shaped by this land over many thousands of years."

Uluru-Kata Tjuta National Park, Australia

Sculthorpe's music reflects the vast loneliness of the Australian **landscape** and his wish to protect it. His work also echoes the **conflict** between early European settlers in Australia and the native Aboriginal population.

The kangaroo is the national symbol of Australia.

Most of the musical pieces by Australian composer Peter Sculthorpe are about the **people** and **landscape** of his home country. He writes all types of music – for orchestra and string quartet as well as choir and opera.

Going back

Sculthorpe often revisits earlier compositions, **reworking** them for different instruments. Some melodies (such as *Djilili*) recur throughout his work. Other pieces are less melodic, such as *Sun Music I*. Sculthorpe wrote several *Sun Music* pieces, later **combining** them to make his *Sun Music* ballet.

Sun Music ballet performed by The Australian Ballet in 1968.

Asian influences
As a young composer, Sculthorpe turned away from the European musical tradition, exploring Asian music and instruments instead. For several years, he taught Indonesian music but found this did not give him enough time to compose.

Sculthorpe playing a Thai drum.

Although a classical guitarist, John Williams also plays jazz and rock music.

John Williams (1941–)

Australian **guitarist** John Williams plays music by composers around the world, including music by Tōru Takemitsu of Japan and Cuba's Leo Brouwer. He also performs pieces by composers from his own country, including Sculthorpe's *Djilili*, based on an Aboriginal melody.

Didgeridoo player William Barton performed in *Requiem* at the 2004 Adelaide Festival, Australia.

Requiem (2004)

Sculthorpe wrote this in memory of his parents and for children who died in wars around the world. His requiem includes drumming, chanting, and **seagull-like cries** (made by stringed instruments). It combines Aboriginal lullaby with orchestra, voice, and the **didgeridoo**.

Today's **new sounds**

What's the next "new thing" for music? In this **electronic** music age, huge music recording companies publicize through the media, so 21st century musicians have the challenge to use the Internet and digital music technology for **do-it-yourself** music production and for experimenting with new sounds.

How did it happen?

In the 1970s, the German band Kraftwerk was one of the first groups to make **electronic music** popular. Influenced by Karlheinz Stockhausen (see page 126) and minimalism, they distorted the sound of the electronic instruments and vocals.

KRAFTWERK (1970–)

From the 1970s, five huge music recording companies dominated the mainstream charts while the "underground" music scene helped to establish experimental groups.

In Germany, **krautrock** bands, such as Can, developed new electronic ideas, while in Britain, **progressive rock** bands, such as King Crimson (shown here), produced "concept albums" – an epic story told through a number of long, skilful instrumental or lyrical tracks.

The first synthesizer-based record to become a hit was Are "Friends" Electric? *performed by Gary Numan and the Tubeway Army in 1979.*

The rock band Nirvana's second album *Nevermind* (1991) was an unexpected success and brought the alternative rock style known as **grunge** into the mainstream. This has been a lasting influence on modern rock music.

NIRVANA (1987–1994)

Since the 1990s, the Internet and availability of digital technology has helped small independent labels (known as indie music) to create and distribute their records.

Synthesizer

Although by the 1980s electronic musical devices were affordable, they were not compatible with those from other manufacturers. In 1982, the MIDI (Musical Instrumental Digital Interface) standard was set. Keyboardists could now control the sound of many different instruments from a single keyboard.

LISTEN TO TRACK 35

Listen for the vocal percussion sounds in this piece of funky electronica.

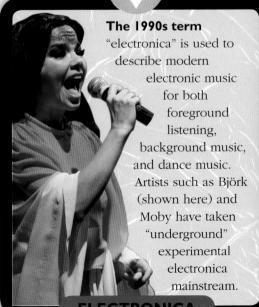

The 1990s term "electronica" is used to describe modern electronic music for both foreground listening, background music, and dance music. Artists such as Björk (shown here) and Moby have taken "underground" experimental electronica mainstream.

ELECTRONICA

21st century musicians continue to take music styles in new directions...

Solo artists

Arkin Ilicali (1966–)
Known as Mercan Dede or DJ Arkin Allen, this Turkish composer is also an accomplished **ney player** and DJ, mixing Turkish and other Asian music and classical instruments with electronic sounds.

Matthias Paul (1971–)
This leading **electronic dance** music DJ is known as Paul van Dyk. His fifth studio album *In Between* included collaborations with David Bryne of Talking Heads and Jessica Sutta of Pussycat Dolls.

Lady Gaga (1986–)
Born Stefani Germanotta, this American recording artist has a very **theatrical** pop style inspired by fashion, 1980s pop, and glam rock singers such as David Bowie and Freddie Mercury.

Bands

Garbage (formed 1994)
Shirley Manson is the Scottish lead singer in this **alternative rock** band of American instrumentalists. Their infectious melodies are created using grungy guitars and distorted electronic sounds.

Little Tragedies (formed 1994)
The concept albums of this Russian **progressive rock** band with their melodic keyboard solos are influenced by classical music and heavy art-rock.

Sigur Rós (formed 1994)
This Icelandic post-rock band produces **ethereal sounding** music and uses classical and minimalist elements, such as orchestral and string arrangements. The lead singer, Jónsi, is known for using a cello bow to play his guitar.

Tokio Hotel (formed 2001)
This German pop rock band experiments with new sounds and subjects. Their single, *Automatic,* is a **metallic anthem** with layered, buzzing guitars, stomping percussion, and a falsetto chorus designed to be belted out by a stadium full of people.

Empire of the Sun (formed 2006)
The Australian music duo, Luke Steele and Nick Littlemore, have a **retro-electronic** pop style. They released six tracks of their debut album *Walking on a Dream* on the social networking site MySpace to promote themselves.

NEW INSTRUMENT

Reactable
This revolutionary instrument is a luminous round table. **Electronic devices**, known as pucks, have different effects such as synthesizers, controllers, and sample loops. When placed on the table, the pucks interact with each other. One or more musicians can turn and move these pucks, creating unique sounds.

Music festivals

All over the world, hordes of music fans descend on venues to hear their favourite performers. Many have grown into huge events, where thousands live in tent cities and the community spirit is a key part.

▲ **Woodstock, New York State, USA**
Held in 1969, this was the first of the big outdoor rock concerts – a key moment in popular music history. Half a million people spent three days in a muddy field listening to the biggest acts of the day, including Joan Baez, Jimi Hendrix, Janis Joplin, and The Who.

▲ **Glastonbury, England** Glastonbury is the UK's largest annual rock concert, featuring more than 700 acts that cover a wide range of different music styles, from Oasis to Jay-Z. It also includes dance, comedy, circus, cabaret, theatre, and many other arts.

▼ **Sziget Festival, Budapest, Hungary**
This mixture of alternative modern music takes place on an island in the Danube River.

▲ **Rock'n Coke, Istanbul, Turkey** At the end of the summer, a two-day rock festival sponsored by Coca Cola is held on the Hezarfen Airfield, where Turkish and international bands perform.

▲ **Fuji Rock, Naeba, Japan** Named after Mount Fuji, where the first festival was held, this is Japan's largest outdoor festival with more than 100,000 people attending.

▲ **Roskilde Festival, Denmark** One of the main summer festivals in northern Europe, Roskilde features a 17,000 capacity arena tent. It has hosted many major artists, from Bob Marley to Bob Dylan.

▼ **Sauti za Busara, Zanzibar, Tanzania** This festival, has been going since 2003. Celebrating the music of East Africa, the whole family is encouraged to enjoy its mixture of modern, classical, acoustic, and electric sounds.

◄ **Salzburg Festival, Austria** Each summer, the city of Salzburg – the birthplace of Mozart – hosts a drama and classical music festival.

▼ **Rabindra Sadan Festival, Calcutta, West Bengal** A seven day annual music festival, featuring thousands of Indian performers, is held at this cultural centre.

Bengal singer Lopamudra

▲ **Rock al Parque, Bogota, Colombia** Originally a rock concert, this event now features punk, reggae, ska, and blues. This is one of a series of festivals. The other festivals celebrate jazz, hip hop, opera, and zarzuela, a type of musical theatre.

Experience the
real *thing!*

Recordings and performances of many of the pieces of classical music and popular songs mentioned in this book can be heard on discs or on websites and downloaded onto your portable players. But **listening to live music** can be very exciting and an experience you may never forget.

YOUR TICKET TO:
A WORLD MUSIC FESTIVAL

Find out about amateur and community musical events happening in parks, churches, and schools near you, listen to a professional orchestra and choir perform at a concert hall, and look up the performers and bands playing at a music festival.

Also why not **get involved** in the experience of making music? Joining a choir, whether large or small, can be great fun and an uplifting experience, and you can get the chance to sing all sorts of classical and popular songs.

Everyone can shake, strum, blow, or hit something to make music. Take this a step further and learn to play an instrument. Ask a musician friend or find a teacher to help you. Also **you too could be a composer**, and so record those tunes that come into your head, or write down your ideas to shape into lyrics. Maybe you have the talent to be a gifted Mozart, an experimental Jimi Hendrix, or a legendary Michael Jackson. Music can change your life.

20th century composer, Michael Tippett, giving a **music workshop** to the string section of a youth orchestra.

Glossary

12-tone music without a key, and in which all the 12 notes of an octave have equal importance.

Acoustic an instrument or type of music that does not use electrical amplification.

Alto a low female singing voice or instrument with a range between soprano and tenor.

Atonal music that has no particular key. Atonal music developed in the 20th century.

Avant-garde radical, ahead-of-its-time music that is different from traditional musical structures.

Ballad a type of narrative folk song that dates back to medieval Europe.

Ballet a graceful dance, with elaborate steps and flowing movements.

Baritone a male singing voice or musical instrument, with a range between tenor and bass.

Bass a male singing voice or musical instrument with the lowest range, below baritone.

Basso continuo (often shortened to "continuo"), where the harmony is improvised around the written bass part of the music.

Blues an emotional musical style that is characterized by slow beats, repeated harmonies, and the use of "blue notes" lowered in pitch so as to express sad feelings.

Boogie-woogie a bluesy piano dance music, characterized by a swinging, syncopated rhythm and a simple, often improvised, melody.

Bossa nova a Brazilian rhythm based on a samba dance, a musical genre with African roots.

Cakewalk a dance with exaggerated walking steps that is performed to marching music.

Canon and fugue pieces in which two or more vocal or instrumental parts performing the same melody are introduced, one after the other, to form a structure of overlapping melodies.

Cantata a type of religious vocal composition performed with instrumental accompaniment.

Chamber music music that is performed by small groups of musicians. Traditionally chamber music was played in small rooms to entertain members of the aristocracy.

Chord a group of notes that are played at the same time.

Concert a public performance of music.

Concerto a piece of music written for a solo instrumentalist with orchestral accompaniment.

Conductor the person who directs an orchestra and makes sure that the timing, volume, and feeling of the music is correct for the piece.

Cyclic form a composition where certain themes or melodies are repeated through several sections. This helps to link the sections together.

Drone a pipe or string instrument that sounds a note, which is held for a long period of time.

Duet a piece of music written for two singers or instrumentalists.

Embouchure the use of the facial muscles and the shaping of the lips to the mouthpiece of a brass or woodwind instrument.

Ensemble a small group of musicians.

Fado a mournful, Portuguese urban folk music.

Flamenco an expressive and passionate Spanish folk dance, coming from the Andalusian region in southern Spain.

Folk music the distinctive music and songs of a people or region. Folk music uses traditional melodies and the songs describe the interests and concerns of the people.

Gospel music a joyful and expressive form of religious music influenced by African American culture, and characterized by jazzy rhythms, strong voices, and lots of harmonizing.

Grunge an alternative style of rock music that is characterized by a raw sound, discordant guitars, and angry or depressed song lyrics.

Harmony the sound created when several notes are played together in chords.

Hymn a religious song that praises God.

Improvisation making up the music spontaneously, whilst playing an instrument or singing.

Jazz an expressive type of music that uses syncopated rhythms and lots of improvisation, and relies on spontaneous creative interaction between the performers.

Key used to describe the tonal setting of a piece of music. The key is based on the main scale in which the music is played.

Lied a type of German song with piano accompaniment. The words are taken from lyrical, romantic poems.

Lyrics the words of a song.

Madrigal choral music written for small groups of singers without musical accompaniment.

Mass a service held by the Roman Catholic Church and the choral music that accompanies it.

Melodrama characterful music that uses spoken voice with instrumental music in the background.

Melody a succession of notes with a recognizable tune.

Minimalist a popular type of experimental music, which uses few musical notes, words, and instruments. Simple elements such as melodies are repeated over and over, producing an hypnotic effect.

Minuet an elegant dance in triple time (three beats in each bar) that became popular in Europe in the 17th century.

Monody music where the melody is sung, and instruments play the chords beneath it.

Monophony music that has a single melody and no accompanying harmony.

Motet a type of religious choral music.

Motif a short arrangement of notes, or a fragment of rhythm, harmony, or melody that is repeated at various points within a composition.

Notation a system used to write down music.

Octave the interval or gap between eight notes on the musical scale. The notes at the top and bottom of an octave share the same letter-name.

Opera a theatrical play that is set to music. All the performers sing their parts and the music is played by an orchestra.

Opus a particular work produced by a composer. A composition may be given an opus number so that it can be easily identified from other works by the same composer.

Oratorio a musical setting of a story (often religious). Although similar to opera, oratorios are not performed with scenery or costumes.

Orchestra a large group of musicians who play music together on various instruments.

Ornaments musical notes that are added for decorative effect.

Ostinato a short tune or rhythm that is frequently repeated within a composition.

Overture the music played at the start of an opera or musical, containing some of the memorable tunes from the main performance.

Patron someone who gives financial assistance to musicians or who uses power or influence on their behalf.

Pick a small device that is used to pluck the strings of musical instruments, such as guitars.

Pitch the description of how high or low a particular note is on the musical scale.

Plainchant a chanted song that follows a simple, single melody. The words are taken from the Roman Catholic Mass and are usually chanted without musical accompaniment.

Polyphony music made up of several melodies.

Polyrhythm music made up of several rhythms.

Polytonal music that uses several tonalities or keys at the same time.

Pop an abbreviation of "popular" music. Pop music changes quickly to reflect changing tastes and is characterized by the simple tunes and strong rhythms that make it catchy or danceable.

Prelude a piece of music that may stand alone or is intended as an introduction to a longer piece.

Premiere the first public performance of a musical composition.

Prodigy someone who shows extraordinary talent and musical ability from a very early age.

Quintet a group of five singers or instrumentalists.

Raga one of many possible selections of notes on which a performance of Indian music is based.

Ragtime an early 20th-century style of piano music that has syncopated rhythm.

Rap music with lyrics that are rapped or chanted against a strong background beat.

Reed a thin piece of wood, metal, or plastic that sits in the mouthpiece of a woodwind instrument.

Requiem a piece of music related to mourning or a religious ceremony in honour of the dead.

Rhythm and blues (R&B) a style of music that combines blues and jazz, with repeated variations on syncopated instrumental phrases.

Riff a constantly repeated series of notes or a chord progression that is played by the rhythm section of a band or a solo instrument.

Rock-and-roll a fusion of rhythm and blues and country music, characterized by a heavy beat, strong rhythm, and repeated musical phrases.

Sonata a piece written for a solo instrument with or without a piano accompaniment, or for solo piano.

Song cycle a group of songs that either tell a story or share a common theme.

Soprano a high female singing voice or a musical instrument with the highest range.

Soul a type of music with intense, soulful lyrics that is heavily influenced by gospel music, but also mixes in elements of blues and rock-and-roll.

Spirituals emotional religious songs that were created by African American slaves.

Sprechstimme an operatic form of expression, which is halfway between speaking and singing.

Stave the set of five horizontal lines on which the score of the music is written.

String quartet a group of four musicians, usually made up of two violinists, a viola player, and a cellist.

Suite a number of short instrumental pieces that can be performed together or independently.

Swing a type of jazz that was developed by big dance band musicians in the 1930s.

Symphonic poem a composition that describes a particular subject, poem, story, character, painting, or landscape in musical form.

Symphony usually a large-scale piece of instrumental music, most often made up of four contrasting sections (movements), that is written for an entire orchestra.

Syncopation a type of rhythm in which the regular pattern of beats is interrupted by stressing the weak beats.

Synthesizer an electronic instrument that produces sound electronically.

Tala the rhythm in Indian classical music.

Tenor a high male singing voice or a musical instrument with a range between alto and baritone.

Tonal music music in a key, or arranged around a particular scale or pitch. This gives the music structure.

Tone also known as timbre, the quality or character of the sound produced by an instrument or voice.

Tone cluster a chord created by simultaneously playing three or more notes that are close together on the musical scale.

Valve the part of a brass instrument that can be used to vary the pitch of the sound produced.

Variations a collection of pieces that are all based on the same theme but where each piece differs in some way.

Virtuoso an outstanding singer or musician.

Word painting when music reflects the meaning of a song. For example, if the lyrics tell of climbing a mountain, the music may use ascending scales.

Index of musicians

141

Acknowledgements

Dorling Kindersley would like to thank Richard Beatty and Lorrie Mack for proofreading and Lee Wilson for further editorial help.

The publisher would like to thank the following for their kind permission to reproduce their photographs:

(Key: a-above; b-below/bottom; c-centre; f-far; l-left; r-right; t-top)

3 Dorling Kindersley: Steinway and Sons. **4-5 Getty Images:** Peter Adams (b). **6 Getty Images:** Graham Wiltshire/Hulton Archive (c). **7 Getty Images:** AFP (c); Francesco Botticini (t); Lisa Maree Williams (b). **8-9 Corbis:** Michael Pole (background). Marshall Amplification plc: Marshall stack image(s) supplied by Marshall Amplification plc – www.marshallamps. com (amplifiers). **10-11 Corbis:** Stapleton Collection. **12 Amgueddfa Cymru – National Museum Wales:** (cra/flint stone). **National Museum of Slovenia:** Tomaž Lauko (cla). **Photolibrary:** Kyle Rothenborg/Pacific Stock (cla). **Science Photo Library:** Sinclair Stammers (b). **12-13 Alamy Images:** Pavel Filatov (bc). **Corbis:** M. Angelo (background). **13 Bryan and Cherry Alexander/ArcticPhoto:** (tl). **Corbis:** Brooklyn Museum (cb); Alain Le Garsmeur (cla). **Getty Images:** Robyn Beck/AFP (br). **14 The Bridgeman Art Library:** Museo della Civiltà Romana, Rome/Roger-Viollet, Paris (l). **Corbis: The Gallery Collection** (crb); Otto Lang (br). **Getty Images:** Roger-Viollet Collection (cra). **15 Alamy Images:** Dinodia Images (cb); The Print Collector (fcla). **The Bridgeman Art Library:** Bibliothèque des arts décoratifs, Paris/Archives Charmet (cla). **The Trustees of the British Museum:** (crb). **Corbis:** Asian Art & Archaeology, Inc. (clb); Roger Wood (tr). With kind permission of Richard Dumbrill, **The Archaeomusicology of the Ancient Near East, Trafford 2005:** (bc). **Flickr.com:** Leslie Lewis (cra). **Getty Images:** The Bridgeman Art Library (tc). **16 Corbis:** Paul A. Souders (cl); Penny Tweedie (tr). **Getty Images:** Penny Tweedie/The Image Bank (br). **Lebrecht Music and Arts:** Chris Stock (b). **16-17 Corbis:** Andrew Watson/JAI (background). **17 Getty Images:** Claire Leimbach (tr); Robert Harding World Imagery (clb). **Lebrecht Music and Arts:** Richard H. Smith (tl). **Photo courtesy RMIT: Photographer:** Jim Mepham (br). **18 Alamy Images:** Hemera Technologies (cl); Edwin Remsberg (cl). **19 Alamy Images:** INTERFOTO (l). **Corbis:** Frans Lemmens (br) (tc/zurna). **Lebrecht Music and Arts:** Museum of Fine Arts, Boston (tl/zummara). **20 Alamy Images:** AfriPics.com (cla/West African frame); Michael Jenner (cr). **Corbis:** Bruno Morandi/Robert Harding World Imagery (fcla). **Getty Images:** Jack Dykinga/The Image Bank (b). **iStockphoto.com:** Roberto Gennaro (cra/ Berber frame). **21 Alamy Images:** Robert Fried (br/Zimbabwe frame); J. Marshall/Tribaleye Images (clb/Buganda frame); Jacques Jangoux (cra/ musicians); Zute Lightfoot (tr/Mozambique frame); Jamie Marshall/Tribal Textiles/Tribaleye Images (tl/Nigeria frame); Chris Stock/Lebrecht Music & Arts (crb); Andrew Woodley (br/East Africa frame). **Corbis:** Anthony Bannister/Gallo Images (bc). **iStockphoto.com:** Thomas Moens (cla). **Lonely Planet Images:** Ariadne Van Zandbergen (tr). **22 Alamy Images:** Lou-Foto (tl). **The Bridgeman Art Library:** Bibliothèque des arts décoratifs, Paris/Archives Charmet (bl/stone chimes and ocarina). **Corbis:** Li Nan/ Redlink (cla/pipa player). **Lebrecht Music and Arts:** Graham Salter (br). **23 Alamy Images:** Aflo Co. Ltd./AM Corporation (br); Classic Image (bl/frame); Franck Guiziou/Hemis (bl/close-up on hand). **Lebrecht Music and Arts:** Paul Tomlins (tl). **24 Dorling Kindersley:** Anthony Barton Collection (clb). **25 Lebrecht Music and Arts:** Museum of Fine Arts, Boston (l/Irish harp). **26 Corbis:** Franz-Marc Frei (cr). **Getty Images:** The Bridgeman Art Library (cr). **iStockphoto.com:** Andrew Howe (tl/bird). **Photo Scala, Florence:** (clb). **27 Alamy Images:** Classic Image (l/frieze). **The Bridgeman Art Library:** Private Collection/Roger Perrin (tl). **Corbis:** Luca Tettoni (ca). **Getty Images:** Pascal Le Segretain (ca); Cristina Quicler/AFP (bl); Jeremy Samuelson (br). **28 Alamy Images:** The Art Gallery Collection/Visual Arts Library (London) (bl). **Photolibrary:** The British Library/Imagestate (cla); Martin Westlake/Asia Images (tl). **28-29 Alamy Images:** Peter Horree (b/ main image). **Getty Images:** Hunghsiang LAN (tr); WorldFoto (tl). **29 Corbis:** EPA/STR (tr); David Lees (tl); Andrew Winning/Reuters (tr). 'The Hippo Man', Mayinda Orawo, Luo tribe, Kenya 1973. Copyright David Fanshawe. Front Cover African Sanctus CD, Silva Records SILKD6003.: (tl). **Lebrecht Music and Arts:** RIA Novosti (br). **31 Alamy Images:** Jon Bower, Oxford (tr). **Corbis:** Anders Ryman (bl). **Getty Images:** Andreas Rentz/Bongarts (br). **Photolibrary:** Karl F. Schöfmann/imagebroker.net (cla). **32 Alamy Images:** V&A Images (cl). **The Bridgeman Art Library:** National Museum of India, New Delhi/Lauros/Giraudon (tl). **32-33 Photolibrary:** Martin Harvey/Peter Arnold Images (main image). **33 Getty Images:** Michael Ochs Archives (br). **iStockphoto.com:** Nikolay Titov (tr/frame). **Sathyadeep Musical Palace:** (cra). **Photolibrary:** The Print Collector/Imagestate (cla); Klaus-Werner Friedrich/imagebroker.net (b). **35 Photograph © 2010 Museum of Fine Arts, Boston:** (cla). **Alamy Images:** Robert M. Vera (bl). **Getty Images:** Diana Ong/Private collection/SuperStock (br). **36-37 Getty Images:** De Agostini Picture Library. **38 Alamy Images:** INTERFOTO (br). **The Bridgeman Art Library:** British Library Board (tl). **Musée Condé, Chantilly, France/Giraudon** (cra/singers). **Corbis:** Bettmann (cb); Stefano Bianchetti (cla); The Gallery Collection (tr). **38-39 Corbis:** Arcaid (columns). **39 The Bridgeman Art Library:** Gemäldegalerie Alte Meister, Dresden/ Staatliche Kunstsammlungen, Dresden (tl); Musée Condé, Chantilly, France/ Lauros/Giraudon (bl). **Corbis:** The Art Archive/A. Dagli Orti (bl); Bettmann (c). **Getty Images:** De Agostini Picture Library/A. Dagli Orti (br); Hulton Archive (cr) (tr). **Lebrecht Music and Arts:** Colouriser AL (bc). **40 Corbis:** Bettmann (tl); Lebrecht Music & Arts (b). **Getty Images:** Hulton Archive (clb). **Wikipedia, The Free Encyclopedia:** (bl). **41 Corbis:** Dave Bartruff (tl); Bettmann (bl); Martin Schutt/DPA (tr). **Getty Images:** Keystone/Hulton Archive (crb). **Corbis:** Christie's Images (tr); Robbie Jack (l); Francis G. Mayer (cra). **42-43 Corbis:** Peter Crowther/Ikon Images (spotlight background). **43 Alamy Images:** RIA Novosti (br). **The Bridgeman Art Library:** Lindenau Museum, Altenburg, Germany/Bildarchiv Foto Marburg (bl). **Corbis:** Hulton-Deutsch Collection (c). **Getty Images:** Hulton Archive (tr) (tl). **Lebrecht Music and Arts:** Tristram Kenton (cl). **44 Corbis:** Bettmann (tl). **Lebrecht Music and Arts:** Wikipedia, The Free Encyclopedia (tl/kobyz). **44-45 Dorling Kindersley:** Stephen Oliver (main violin). **45 Alamy Images:** Graham Salter/Lebrecht Music and Arts (tl). **Corbis:** Stefano Bianchetti (bl). **Getty Images:** Carl De Souza/AFP (cr); Roberto Serra/Iguana Press (bl); Denise Truscello/WireImage (br). **46 Alamy Images:** The Art

Archive (cb/music score). **The Bridgeman Art Library:** Museo di Strumenti del Conservatorio, Naples (cra). **Corbis:** The Art Archive/A. Dagli Orti (tr); Austrian Archives (r); Bettmann (crb). **Getty Images:** PALM/RSCH/Redferns (clb). **Lebrecht Music and Arts:** Colouriser AL (cl). **46-47 Getty Images:** Nicholas Eveleigh/Photodisc (picture frame). **47 Alamy Images:** Mary Evans Picture Library (cr); INTERFOTO (br). **The Bridgeman Art Library:** National Gallery of Victoria, Melbourne/Everard Studley Miller Bequest (tr). **Corbis:** Bettmann (cl); Gianni Dagli Orti (tl). **Getty Images:** Kean Collection/Hulton Archive (tc); ND/Roger Viollet (bl). **Lebrecht Music and Arts:** Colouriser AL (c). **Mary Evans Picture Library:** Grosvenor Prints (bc). **48 Alamy Images:** Lebrecht Music and Arts (tr). **Corbis:** The Art Archive/A. Dagli Orti (clb). **Getty Images:** The Bridgeman Art Library/ Staatliches Museum, Schwerin, Germany (tl). **Photo Scala, Florence:** Foto Austrian Archive (cr). **49 Corbis:** Christie's Images (bl/fortepiano). **Lebrecht Music and Arts:** (cl). **Photo Scala, Florence:** White Images (tr). **50 Alamy Images:** INTERFOTO (cr) (bc). **Corbis:** The Art Archive (t). **Getty Images:** Sean Gallup (clb); Christian Ludwig Seehas/The Bridgeman Art Library (bl). **51 The Bridgeman Art Library:** Beethoven Haus, Bonn/Giraudon (cl); English Heritage. NMR (t). **Lebrecht Music and Arts:** Colouriser AL (c). **52 Adams Musical Instruments, Holland:** (tc/tubular bells). **Dorling Kindersley:** Stephen Oliver (br/violins). **Getty Images:** Stockbyte (tr/tubular bells). **53 Adams Musical Instruments, Holland:** (tl). **Lebrecht Music and Arts:** Chris Stock (ca/bass trombone). **54 Corbis:** The Art Archive/A. Dagli Orti (clb) (tr); Christie's Images (br/painting); The Gallery Collection (cr/Paganini). **Getty Images:** Hulton Archive (ca/Louis Spohr). **iStockphoto.com:** (bl/ feather); Viktor Pravdica (bl/music paper with ink & rose) (br/Weber). **Lebrecht Music and Arts:** (cla). **55 Getty Images:** Lebrecht Music and Arts (tr). **Corbis:** The Art Archive/A. Dagli Orti (tc); Bettmann (br); Michael Nicholson (bc); W. and D. Downey/Hulton Archive (cr). **Getty Images:** Imagno/Hulton Archive (tl) (bl) (cl); Rischgitz/Hulton Archive (c). **56 Alamy Images:** Lebrecht Music and Arts (c). **Corbis:** The Art Archive (fbl); Austrian Archives (fclb). **Getty Images:** Hulton Archive (t). **57 Adams Musical Instruments, Holland:** (tr). **Dorling Kindersley:** Stephen Oliver (crb/violin). **Getty Images:** Apic/Hulton Archive (cb). **Mary Evans Picture Library:** (tr). **58 Corbis:** Robbie Jack (bl). **Getty Images:** Henrietta Butler/ Redferns (cl); Patrick Riviere (br). **Lebrecht Music and Arts:** Private Collection (tl). **58-59 Corbis:** Svenja-Foto (background). **Getty Images:** Paula Bronstein (br). **59 ArenaPAL:** Clive Barda (tl). **Getty Images:** Jacques M. Chenet (t); Historical Picture Archive (r). **Lebrecht Music and Arts:** Heikki Tuuli (cr). **60 Corbis:** The Art Archive (clb). **Getty Images:** De Agostini Picture Library/A. Dagli Orti (bl); Hulton Archive (t). **Lebrecht Music and Arts:** S. Lauterwasser (bl). **61 Corbis:** Photolibrary (cl); Joerg Schulze/EPA (cla). **Getty Images:** Hulton Archive (crb); Three Lions/Hulton Archive (t). **62 Corbis:** (cl) (cla/harpsichord). **Lebrecht Music and Arts:** Museum of Fine Arts, Boston (cla/clavichord). **62-63 Corbis:** Envision (main piano). **63 Alamy Images:** Lebrecht Music and Arts (br); INTERFOTO (tc). **64 Corbis:** Fukuhara, Inc. (br). **Getty Images:** Carlos Alvarez (clb). **65 ArenaPAL:** Boosey & Hawkes Collection (tr). **Corbis:** Latin Stock Collection (cr); George Logan (tr); Rick Rickman/NewSport (tl). **Lebrecht Music and Arts:** Dee Conway (tl) (b). **66 Alamy Images:** Lebrecht Music and Arts (t) (bl). **Getty Images:** Sean Gallup (clb). **66-67 Corbis:** Rune Hellestad (tr). **67 Corbis:** Nir Elias/Reuters (tc). **Getty Images:** Liz Hafalia/San Francisco Chronicle (bl). **68 Alamy Images:** V&A Images (cra/British nationalism frame). **The Bridgeman Art Library:** Museo Nacional de Antropología, Mexico City/Bildarchiv Steffens Henri Stierlin (bc). **Getty Images:** Leon Neal/AFP (cr). **iStockphoto.com:** bernardo69 (br/Central and South American); Nic Taylor (l/American nationalism frame). **Lebrecht Music and Arts:** (cl). **69 akg-images:** Coll. Archiv f. Kunst & Geschichte (cl). **Alamy Images:** RIA Novosti (cr). **Corbis:** The Gallery Collection (bl); Paul Seheult/Eye Ubiquitous (crb). **ibsen.net:** Dana Smillie (tl). **iStockphoto.com:** Thorbjørn Kongshavn (cla/Scandinavian nationalism frame); Ela Kwasniewski (cra/French nationalism frame); naphtalina (bl/ Spanish nationalism frame); Yura Nosenko (tr/Russian nationalism frame); Radu Razvan (br/East European nationalism frame). **70 The Bridgeman Art Library:** Archives Charmet (bl). **Corbis:** Bettmann (clb). **Getty Images:** Frans Lemmens/The Image Bank (t). **Lebrecht Music and Arts:** (c). **71 Alamy Images:** INTERFOTO (tr). **The Bridgeman Art Library:** The Moscow State Conservatory, Russia (cra). **Corbis:** Robbie Jack (c). **Getty Images:** Redferns (tl) (cla). **Lebrecht Music and Arts:** (ca) (br). **72 Corbis:** Bettmann (t); Barry Lewis (br). **Getty Images:** Imagno/Hulton Archive (clb); Hulton Archive (bl). **73 Corbis:** Henny Abrams/Bettmann (tl); Robbie Jack (bl); Michael Ochs Archives (cb). **Lebrecht Music and Arts:** (br). **NASA:** (ca/astronaut). **74 Corbis:** Bettmann (cla) (bl); Hulton-Deutsch Collection (tr); M. Lawn/Hulton-Deutsch Collection (bc); Lebrecht Music & Arts (ca). **74-75 Getty Images:** Henry Wolf/Hulton Archive (background). **75 Corbis:** Angel Medina G./EPA (tl); Robbie Jack (crb) (br) (cra); Leon/Retna Digital (clb). **Getty Images:** Emmanuel Dunand/AFP (br). **Lebrecht Music and Arts:** T. Martinot (c); Royal Academy of Music (r/baton). **76 Corbis:** Sandro Vannini (fcla). **Dorling Kindersley:** Anthony Barton Collection (ca/horn). **77 Alamy Images:** C. Christodoulou/Lebrecht Music & Arts (tr); Powerhouse Digital Photography Ltd. (ca). **Corbis:** Bradley Smith (r). **78 Alamy Images:** Powerhouse Digital Photography Ltd. (cra). **Corbis:** Walter Bibikow/JAI (cla); Dallas and John Heaton/Free Agents Limited (tl). **Lebrecht Music and Arts:** Museum of Fine Arts, Boston (ca). **79 Corbis:** Bettmann (bc). **Lebrecht Music and Arts:** Graham Salter (bl). **80 Corbis:** The Art Archive/A. Dagli Orti (cra). **The Bridgeman Art Library** (bl). **Lebrecht Music and Arts:** (r). **Photo Scala, Florence:** White Images (t). **81 Lebrecht Music and Arts:** (bl) (br) (t). **Photo Scala, Florence:** White Images (cl). **82 Getty Images:** AFP (t); GAB Archive/Redferns (bl); STR/AFP (br). **Lebrecht Music and Arts:** Leemage (clb). **83 Alamy Images:** Gary Cook (t/forest); John Warburton-Lee Photography (tl/Amazon River). **Corbis:** Sunset Boulevard (br). **Arthur Grosset:** (tc/bird). **Lebrecht Music and Arts:** (bl). **84 Corbis:** Lee Snider/Photo Images (b). **Getty Images:** AFP (tr); Redferns (ca). **84-85 iStockphoto.com:** i-bob (background). **85 akg-images:** (tl). **Corbis:** Bettmann (tr). **Getty Images:** Jacques Demarthon/AFP (tr); Kurt Hutton/Picture Post/Hulton Archive (tl); Patrick Riviere (cra). **86-87 Corbis:** Michael Ochs Archives. **88 akg-images:** © ADAGP, Paris and DACS, London 2010/Private Collection (fbl). **Corbis:** Bettmann (cl). **Getty Images:** Laurie Lewis (br) (cra). **89 akg-images:** © DACS 2010/Estate of Heinrich Jalowetz, courtesy of Galerie St. Etienne, New York (cra). **Getty Images:** Hulton Archive (br).

iStockphoto.com: Chris Scredon (tr/canvas). **Lebrecht Music and Arts:** (fcra). **Arnold Schoenberg Institute** (bl/score). **91 Alamy Images:** Judith Collins (bl). **JTB Photo Communications, Inc.** (tl). **Odile Noel/Lebrecht Music and Arts Photo Library** (cr). **Getty Images:** Photodisc/C Squared Studios (cb). **92 Alamy Images:** Mary Evans Picture Library (cla/plantation); North Wind Picture Archives (crb/freed slaves); Pictorial Press Ltd (br) (cra/slave trade). **Corbis:** Bettmann (bl). **Duke University:** Rare Book, Manuscript, and Special Collections Library (ca). **93 Alamy Images:** Pictorial Press Ltd (tl). **Getty Images:** Alan Band/Fox Photos/Photoshot/Hulton Archive (tr); Tom Copi/Michael Ochs Archives (bc); David Redfern (br); Hulton Archive (tc); Michael Ochs Archives (c); Leni Sinclair/Michael Ochs Archives (c). **Photo courtesy of Proper Records Ltd:** (tl). **94 Getty Images:** MPI (tl). **United States Postal Service:** (br). **95 Corbis:** Bettmann (tr); Minnesota Historical Society (crb); Frank Driggs Collection/Archive Photos (tl). **Getty Images:** Frank Driggs Collection (bc) (ca); Gjon Mili/Time Life Pictures (tr). **iStockphoto.com:** Joachim Angeltun (b/piano keys). **Lebrecht Music and Arts:** Odile Noël (bl); Rue des Archives (br). **96 Alamy Images:** Pictorial Press Ltd (b). **The Bridgeman Art Library:** Giraudon (tl). **Getty Images:** Markus Amon (clb); Pierre Petit/Hulton Archive (tr). **97 Lebrecht Music and Arts:** Graham Salter (tl). **98 Getty Images:** Ted Foxx (cb). **Corbis:** Erich Auerbach/Hulton-Deutsch Collection (b). **Getty Images:** Keystone/Hulton Archive (cra); Luis Magan/Cover/Hulton Archive (t); Travelpix Ltd/Photographer's Choice (bl). **99 Corbis:** Mike Kemp/Rubberball (r/braille background). **Getty Images:** Erich Auerbach/Hulton Archive (cb); Luis Magan/Cover/Hulton Archive (cra). **Photolibrary:** AGERM-00066734-001 (cla). **Press Association Images:** DPA Deutsche Press-Agentur/DPA (cb/braille reading). **100 Corbis:** Bettmann (cla) (bl) (br). **Dorling Kindersley:** The Science Museum, London (tr). **Duke University:** Rare Book, Manuscript, and Special Collections Library (cl). **100-101 iStockphoto.com:** Maksym Yemelynov (background). **101 Corbis:** Peter Lorimer/EPA (crb); Michael Ochs Archives (c); Shepard Sherbell (bl). **Getty Images:** Larry Busacca/WireImage (br); Michael Ochs Archives (tl) (tr); Courtesy of Sony Music Entertainment/Michael Ochs Archives (clb). **102 Corbis:** Bettmann (tl); Walter Bibikow/JAI (tr); Underwood & Underwood (bl); Gene Lester/Hulton Archive (c); Michael Ochs Archives (bc); Popperfoto (bl). **103 Corbis:** Bettmann (c). **Getty Images:** AFP (cr); Santi Visalli Inc./Archive Photos (cl). **104 Alamy Images:** JTB Photo Communications, Inc. (ca). **Getty Images:** Museum of the City of New York/Archive Photos (bl). **Lebrecht Music and Arts:** Tristram Kenton (br). **104-105 iStockphoto.com:** i-bob (background). **105 Alamy Images:** Chris Davies (t); Pictorial Press Ltd (tl). **Getty Images:** AFP (bl); Time & Life Pictures (tr); Roger Viollet (cr); WireImage (br). **106 Corbis:** Michael Ochs Archives (tl). **Getty Images:** Michael Ochs Archives (bl); Redferns (fbl) (cl); Courtesy of Sony Music Entertainment/Michael Ochs Archives (r). **107 Getty Images:** Fotos International/Archive Photos (br); Michael Ochs Archives (l) (c). **108 Getty Images:** Blank Archives/ Hulton Archive (cla/badges); © Apple Corps Ltd./Michael Ochs Archives (t); Keystone/Hulton Archive (clb/Everly Brothers); NY Daily News (bc); Michael Ochs Archives (clb/Buddy Holly). **108-109 Lebrecht Music and Arts:** David Farrell (bc). **109 Getty Images:** Hulton Archive (tl). **110 Corbis:** Bojan Brecelj (cr); Neal Preston (br); David Corio/Michael Ochs Archives (cb). **Getty Images:** David Corio/Redferns (ca); Tim Hall/Redferns (cr); Michael Ochs Archives (tr/band). **iStockphoto.com:** ayzek (tr/flag). **111 Alamy Images:** Archives du 7ème Art/Photos 12 (tr); Pictorial Press Ltd (tl). **Corbis:** Debra Trebitz (bc); David Corio/Redferns (tc). **Getty Images:** David Corio/Michael Ochs Archives (cr); Mark Metcalfe (br); Tim Mosenfelder (bl); Bernd Muller/Redferns (cl); Mike Prior/Redferns (tc). **112 Getty Images:** Annamaria DiSanto/WireImage (cr). **iStockphoto.com:** Anton Gvozdikov (br). **113 Getty Images:** Walter Iooss Jr (tl); Martin Philbey/Redferns (bc). **iStockphoto.com:** Reid Harrington (tc); Illych (crb/metallic surface). **114 Getty Images:** Colin Fuller/Redferns (bl); GAB Archive/Redferns (tl/album cover). **LedZeppelin.com:** (t); P. Carrey (clb). **114-115 Corbis:** Neal Preston (main image). **115 Getty Images:** Michael Ochs Archives (br); Graham Wiltshire/Hulton Archive (bl). **116 Getty Images:** GAB Archive/Redferns (c); Michael Ochs Archives (cra) (crb); Popperfoto (clb); Gus Stewart/ Redferns (br). **iStockphoto.com:** James Steidl (cl). **Photolibrary:** Foto Beck (tr). **116-117 iStockphoto.com:** julichka (record). **117 Corbis:** Bettmann (tl). **Getty Images:** AFP (br); Photo by Dick Zimmerman ©1982 MJJ Productions, Inc./GAB Archive/Redferns (c); Ralf Juergens (cr); Chiaki Nozu (bl); Jack Robinson (tc); Jason Squires/WireImage (tl); Chris Walter/ WireImage (br). **Rex Features:** Everett Collection (tr). **118 Corbis:** Bernard Bisson/Sygma (l); Mohamed Messara/EPA (tr). **Lebrecht Music and Arts:** African Pictures (cr). **118-119 Corbis:** John Watkins/Frank Lane Picture Agency (zebra pattern background). **119 Getty Images:** Mike Hutchings/Reuters (br); Neal Preston (br); Reuters (t). **Lebrecht Music and Arts:** Paul Tomlins (tr) (cr); Gerry Walden (ca). **120 Alamy Images:** PYMCA (clb). **Corbis:** Carol Friedman (cr). **Getty Images:** David Corio/Redferns (br); Sean Gallup (bl); Peter Kramer (c); Al Pereira/WireImage (crb). **PYMCA.com:** Henry Iddon (cra/DJ Kool Herc). **121 Alamy Images:** PYMCA (tc). **Corbis:** Henry Diltz (cr); Lawrence Manning (tl); Picture Hooked/Loop Images (c). **Getty Images:** Scott Gries (cra); Leo Vals/Hulton Archive (bl); Bruno Vincent (bc). **PYMCA.com:** Fela (br). **122 Corbis:** Philippe Body/Hemis (br). **Getty Images:** Picture Post/Hulton Archive (cr). **Mosfilm Cinema Concern:** (cr). **The Ronald Grant Archive:** Dispat Films (cr). **122-123 iStockphoto.com:** Marcela Barsse (reel background). **The Kobal Collection:** 20th Century Fox/Matt Groening (cb); Columbia/Sony/Chan Kam Chuen (t). **The Ronald Grant Archive:** 20th Century Fox/Lucasfilms (bl); Canal+/Riofilmes (bl). **124 Corbis:** Frédéric Soltan/Sygma (br). **Getty Images:** Dave Benett (cl); Jason Kempin/WireImage for Time Inc. (t/A.R. Rahman); Michael Ochs Archives (bl/Jim Reeves); H. K. Rajashekar/The India Today Group (bc). **Reuters:** Fred Prouser (r). **125 Alamy Images:** Photos 12/Archives du 7eme Art (fcrb); John Henry Claude Wilson/Robert Harding Picture Library Ltd (cr). **Corbis:** Tim Mosenfelder (cr). **Getty Images:** Sipra Das/India Today Group (cla). **The Kobal Collection:** Film 4/Celador Films/Pathe International (crb). **Press Association Images:** Matt Sayles (ca). **The Ronald Grant Archive:** (bl). **126 Alamy Images:** Will Pryce/Thames & Hudson/Arcaid (bl); Chris Stock/Lebrecht Music & Arts (cr). **The Bridgeman Art Library:** Private Collection/Roger-Viollet, Paris (cra). **Corbis:** Lebrecht Music & Arts (cla); Sylvia Salmi/Sygma (bl/Schoenberg). **Getty Images:** Jorg Greuel/ Photonica (tr/TV); Popperfoto (br). **Lebrecht Music and Arts:** Leemage (crb). **127 Corbis:** Christopher Felver (tl). **Getty Images:** Erich Auerbach/